This book belongs
to
audrey

FOR HORSE-CRAZY GIRLS ONLY

EVERYTHING YOU ✿ WANT ✿ TO ✿ KNOW ✿ ABOUT ✿ HORSES

BY CHRISTINA WILSDON   ILLUSTRATED BY ALECIA UNDERHILL

FEIWEL AND FRIENDS

NEW YORK

For Sophie Jean, my own horse-crazy girl —C.W.

To Michael, Max, and the special horses in my life—
Unique, Ambition, and Heather —A.U.

A FEIWEL AND FRIENDS BOOK
An Imprint of Macmillan

Printed in the United States of America by
R. R. Donnelley & Sons Company, Crawfordsville, Indiana.
For information, address Feiwel and Friends, 175 Fifth Avenue, New York, N.Y. 10010.

Library of Congress Cataloging-in-Publication Data

Wilsdon, Christina.
For horse-crazy girls only : everything you want to know about horses /
Christina Wilsdon. — 1st ed.
p. cm.
Includes bibliographical references and index.
ISBN: 978-0-312-60323-6
1. Horses—Juvenile literature. I. Title.
SF302.W534 2010   636.1—dc22   2010015677

Edited by Susan Bishansky
Book design by Barbara Grzeslo

Feiwel and Friends logo designed by Filomena Tuosto

First Edition: 2010

10 9 8

mackids.com

Dear Horse-Crazy Girls,

When I was a little girl, I wasn't able to have a horse of my own, but I never let that get in the way of my obsession with horses. I loved everything about them—and I still do!

From collecting Breyer models to reading classics like *Misty of Chincoteague* and *The Black Stallion*, to watching movies like *National Velvet* and *The Man from Snowy River*, I kept my love of horses alive by surrounding myself with horsey things and reading everything I could about them.

This passion for horses led me to pursue a career in the horse industry, where I've enjoyed a variety of positions in journalism, marketing, and product development for companies such as the American Horse Shows Association (now USEF—United States Equestrian Foundation) and Breyer. It's been wonderful to work with my favorite subject—the horse—every day, and earn a living doing so!

That's why I'm so excited to share *For Horse-Crazy Girls Only* with you—because now you have the opportunity to make horses a part of your everyday world, too. The author, Christina Wilsdon, has compiled an AMAZING collection of equine information—facts, fictions, and lore. She was guided and helped in this endeavor by her own horse-crazy girl, Sophie, and by all the horse-crazy girls (now grown up) here at Breyer. This fun, fact-filled book about horses was beautifully illustrated by another horse-crazy gal, Alecia Underhill.

For Horse-Crazy Girls Only has lots of great stuff about all things horsey, and I especially love all the engaging sidebars and facts that Chris has assembled. I know that every member of our team here at Breyer learned something from it that they didn't know before.

So, from all the horse-crazy staff at Breyer, we hope you enjoy this wonderful book and its fantastic illustrations.

Keep your horse dreams alive, and enjoy the ride!

Stephanie Macejko
Vice President of Marketing
Breyer

✻ Contents ✻✻✻

WHAT'S SO GREAT ABOUT HORSES (and being a horse-crazy girl)?

If you're reading this book, you're probably a horse-crazy girl.

And if you *are* horse crazy, you know just why horses are so great! They're beautiful. And fast. And lovely to watch, whether they're grazing peacefully or galloping with manes and tails flying.

Horses can become your friends, too. They're social animals, so they like hanging around with their pals—other horses as well as you! And because they're social, they pick up on how other horses feel, and they can also sense your mood.

Horses are smart, and their memory is excellent. If you win the friendship of a horse, you've got a friend for life! That's a big responsibility. Both humbling and empowering. But if you click with the horse, you'll just feel right together.

Riding horses is an experience in itself. But being horse crazy isn't just about riding horses. That wouldn't explain why horse-crazy girls draw them, hang around them, read about them, and muck out their stalls. It's a life-long adventure.

Being horse crazy will surely lead you down some bridle trails, but it can also take you on many other paths, too. It took me on a path to being a writer, and to writing this book.

You can read *For Horse-Crazy Girls Only* in any order. Just open the book and jump to whatever topic grabs your interest first.

I hope this book inspires you to follow your own horse-filled dreams, and to become the best *you* that you can be.

From one horse-crazy gal (now all grown up and still horse crazy!) to another,

—*Christina Wilsdon*

P.S. I thought that this book wouldn't be complete without a little input from an actual horse-crazy girl still growing up! So you'll see comments from my young teenage daughter, Sophie, throughout the book. She didn't share my enthusiasm for horses right out of the starting gate (when she was two and I urged her to hop aboard a little pony named Rhubarb, she gave me a Look and said, "YOU ride the pony"). But it wasn't long before she chose to be enchanted by horses after all. She started riding when she was six, and she now volunteers as a groom and helper at the stable where she takes lessons.

 are you horse crazy?

Lots of girls like horses. Lots of girls may even say they *love* horses. But how do you know if you've gone off the edge into "horse crazy"? Simple: Just take this quiz and find out! Query your horsey friends, too.

1. Your first favorite animal is a horse. Your second is
   a. a dog
   b. a cat
   c. a horse

2. The last three books you read for fun were about
   a. romance
   b. vampires
   c. horses

3. Your bedroom walls are covered with posters. Most of them are pictures of
   a. celebrities
   b. kittens
   c. horses

4. It drives you crazy when
   a. you can't find matching socks
   b. your favorite breakfast cereal is all gone
   c. you see a picture in a horse book that has the bridle straps in all the wrong places: What's up with that?

5. Which of the following statements is true about you?
   a. "I'd rather vacuum than muck out a stall."
   b. "I'd rather clean the cat's litter box than muck out a stall."
   c. "I'd rather muck out a stall than clean my room."

6. Most of the shelf space in your room that isn't devoted to books is given over to
   a. your collection of nail-polish colors
   b. your doll collection
   c. your model-horse collection

7. Every year, your holiday gift wish list has this in the number-one position:
   a. new clothes
   b. a Wii
   c. a horse

8. The margins of your notebooks are filled with doodled drawings of
   a. poodles
   b. flowers
   c. horses

9. You think horses smell
   a. horrible
   b. kind of musty
   c. great

10. Why might somebody say you have a "good seat"?
   a. because they're being rude
   b. because they like your chair
   c. because you ride well

11. The first thing that comes to mind when you think of a halter is
   a. a kind of skimpy shirt
   b. someone who tells you not to run in the hall
   c. headgear for a horse

12. If a friend borrowed one of your T-shirts, chances are that it would sport a picture of
   a. a daisy
   b. a naughty monkey
   c. a horse

Are most (if not all) of your answers "c"? If so, you are certifiably, undeniably, irrefutably, positively, emphatically, definitely, absolutely, unquestionably, totally hopelessly horse crazy!

Your Dream Horse

There isn't a horse-crazy girl anywhere who doesn't dream about the horse she'll have someday.

What does your dream horse look like? Have you ever drawn or painted a picture of it, or written about it? What would you name it? Give your dream horse a personality—with its individual likes and dislikes. Imagine a "back story" for your horse—the story of its life before it met you.

Then, just for fun, check out www.dreamhorse.com. These horses are actually for sale, so don't go writing to their owners! Only those who are really going to buy a horse should do that. *But a girl can dream*—and you can study the horses online as much as you wish to see if one is your dream come true!

are you crazy about . . . Caballos?

Picture this: you're a horse-crazy girl, and you're in a country where people speak a language other than English. How are you going to find a horse? Well, you *could* follow a set of hoof prints, but there's an easier way: Learn how to say "horse" in different languages! Here are a few of the words used around the world to name your favorite four-legged friend.

- Chinese: *mǎ* ("ma-ah")
- French: *cheval* ("shef-ahl")
- German: *Pferd* ("Pff-aired")
- Irish: *capall* ("KAH-puhl")
- Italian: *cavallo* ("CA-vahl-o")
- Japanese: *uma* ("oo-ma")
- Lakota Sioux: *sunka wakan* ("shoo-ka-wa-KAH")
- Portuguese: *cavalo* ("CA-vahl-o")
- Spanish: *caballo* ("ca-VAHL-yo")
- Swedish: *häst* ("hest")

HOW MANY HORSES ARE THERE?

The world's total horse population numbers about 58,370,000, according to a recent study by the United Nations. The United States leads the world in number of horses with about 9.5 million. China comes in second with about 7.4 million. Canada is home to about 453,900 horses.

Happiness Is... Horses!

Top Ten Horse Breeds

Listed here in A-to-Z order are ten of the most popular horse breeds in North America.

A breed's popularity is based on how many horses are registered with an official breed organization. Of these breeds, the quarter horse has the largest breed registry.

American Paint

Appaloosa

Arabian

Miniature Horse

Morgan

Quarter Horse

Saddlebred

Standardbred

Tennessee Walking Horse

Thoroughbred

Popular pony breeds include Shetland, Welsh, and Pony of the Americas.

You can find out more about each breed in any great horse-breed book. You can also learn more online by doing a search using the breed's name plus the words "registry" or "association."

Is your favorite horse missing from the top-ten list? Get together with your horse-crazy friends and make up your own.

A Foal Is Born

A mare in foal carries her baby for about 340 days, or 11 months. The foal is usually born in spring, when new grass is growing and the days are getting warmer. It stands up on its long, wobbly legs and totters to its mother's side before it's even one hour old. Within a day, it can walk, and run, fast enough to keep up with its mom.

At first, the foal drinks only its mother's milk. It starts nibbling grass when it's about six weeks old. When the foal is six months old, it's ready to be "weaned," or separated from its mom. By this time, a broodmare is pregnant with her next foal—so her current foal needs to be on its own before the new one arrives.

When the foal is a year old, it's called a yearling. A yearling foal knows how to behave when it's led by a person on foot or riding a horse. It also learns "good manners" so that it can be tied up, groomed, and handled all over without fussing about being touched.

Training a horse to carry a rider is a long process, which actually begins when the foal is born! A foal should be "gentled" (handled by people) from the

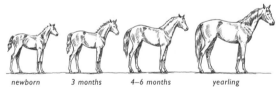

newborn   3 months   4–6 months   yearling

beginning and "halter broke" as a weanling. It's important to gradually introduce it to new situations to create positive experiences and build trust. Depending on the breed, real training begins between the time the horse is a yearling and two years old, when it's introduced to the bridle and saddle. Once comfortable with that, the two-year-old is "backed" (that is, introduced to the concept of carrying a rider). It may carry its first rider when it's about two years old, depending on the breed. If not, it will learn to do that as a three-year-old. (Thoroughbred racehorses are taught at a faster pace so they can be raced as two-year-olds.)

At the age of four, the young horse is fully grown. With good care, it may live to be twenty-five years old or even older.

Dreaming Up a Horse's Name

Many horse-crazy girls like to keep lists of
names they could use for their future
horses (or model horses, or to name
their horses online).

Where to start? You probably
already have thought up some
great names, but here are a few
ideas just in case your imagination
could use some giddy-up:

Books and Myths: Name your horse after a
   famous steed in literature or mythology. Examples: Misty, Black Beauty,
   Flicka, Snowfire, Firefoot.

Foods: Even the grocery store can provide inspiring names.
   ◆**Spices and Herbs** Angelica, Nutmeg, Sassafras.
   ◆**Beverages** Coffee, Chicory, Soda Pop, Cocoa.
   ◆**Treats and Sweets** Cookie, Lollipop, Chocolate Chip, Tutti-Frutti.

Colors: Your choice will likely be inspired by your horse's actual color.
   Examples: Honey, Amber, Copper, Ember.

Stars, Moons, Constellations, and Planets: You'll find all kinds of
   beautiful names in a star guide or a book about astronomy. Examples:
   Vega, Triton, Lyra, Jupiter.

Field Guides: Flip through the pages of a field guide to rocks, birds, fish,
   butterflies, and the like to find some amazing names. Examples: Agate,
   Chickadee, Raven, Coho, Red Admiral, Whirlabout.

Gemstones: Stones used for jewelry inspire many a horse's name.
   Examples: Topaz, Opal, Zircon, Jasper, Ruby.

Towns and Cities: Pore over a map of North America and you'll find many
   perfect names for horses. (You can "travel" farther and look at world
   maps, also.) Examples: Mystic, Plymouth, Eureka, Starbuck.

Days and Months: The calendar can inspire, too. Examples: Saturday, June.

Personality Traits: Is your horse a mischief maker? Is she gentle and kind,
   or fiery? Your horse's temperament can inspire a name. Examples: Pixie,
   Mischief, Thunder, Flame, Sweetie.

Two Words: Sometimes two words are better than one. Examples:
   April Showers, Golden Starlight, Silver Sparkle, Stormy Sky.

Plants: Daffodil, Larkspur, Zinnia, Juniper, Sparkleberry, Willow, Lilac.

Why Racehorses Have Weird Names

Would you ever name your horse Poopydoodle, Snooty Patooty, or Fuzzyheadedlizard? These strange names were all given to real racehorses.

Why do people give odd names to these beautiful animals? One reason is that no two racehorses can share a name, or even have names that sound too much alike. This helps prevent mistaking one horse for another.

Every North American racehorse must have its name approved by the Jockey Club, which has a list of rules that owners must follow. One rule limits a name to 18 letters (this 18-character limit includes spaces between words).

With about 450,000 active names on the books, and thousands of Thoroughbred foals needing new names every year, you can see why you have to think hard to come up with a name that will be one of a kind.

Every year, the Jockey Club prints a list of old names that are available to be used again— so most names do eventually get recycled. You can check out those recently released names online at the Jockey Club's website: www.jockeyclub.com. Click on the link that takes you to their Registry, then look for "Recently Released Names." But some names may be off-limits even after a horse retires.

For example, the Jockey Club keeps a list of permanent names that can never be used again because they belonged to champions who won big races or awards. So you can't name your racer "Man o' War" or "Curlin," for example.

> **Sophie Says:** Here's how I choose horse names: I think of elements in nature—the weather, mountains, or planets—or I think of cities. (I once rode a horse named Redmond, a city in Washington.) My favorites are Willow, Kali, Shasta, Tundra, Blizzard, and Copper.

Top Ten Popular Horse Names IN NORTH AMERICA

Listed here from A to Z are ten popular names for horses, based on Internet searches and an informal survey of riders and riding instructors. Do you know any horses with these names?

- Beau
- Blaze
- Buddy
- Charlie
- Duke
- Ginger
- Harley
- Misty
- Smoky
- Sugar

Top Ten Popular Pony Names IN GREAT BRITAIN

- Beauty
- Billy
- Blackie
- Bobby
- Misty
- Molly
- Monty
- Patch
- Puzzle
- Snowy

Horse Talk

Every subject in the world has its own special vocabulary, and the topic "horse" is no exception.

For starters, there are about four hundred horse breeds and dozens of ways to describe those horses' colors. Add to that the many different kinds of bridles, bits, saddles, and harnesses, as well as riding terms and body parts—and you've got enough words to print a horse dictionary!

But don't bother—it's already been done! Look up one of the 6,600-plus words in *The Horse Dictionary* by Vivienne M. Eby, or go for *The Visual Dictionary of the Horse* by DK Publishing. Online, you can check out an equine dictionary at www.ultimatehorsesite.com/dictionary/dictionary.html.

Since we can't include 6,600 horse words here, we'll just start you off with some of the most common and useful horse terms you'll come across in this book. Being a horse-crazy girl, you may already know some of them!

Horsey Words

Breed: a kind of horse

Broodmare: a female horse used for breeding

Colt: a male horse under the age of four

Dam: the mother of a horse

Draft horse: a tall, heavy-boned horse with strong hindquarters that is often used for pulling plows or heavy loads; the Shire, Clydesdale, and Percheron are examples of draft breeds

Filly: a female horse under the age of four

Foal: a baby horse

Gait: the way a horse moves; walk, trot, and gallop are examples of gaits

Gelding: a neutered male horse. (Stallions can be gelded at any age.)

Harness: equipment worn by a horse pulling a plow, wagon, or carriage

Mare: a female horse four years old or older

Near side: a horse's left side

Off side: a horse's right side

Points: the horse's mane, tail, nose, and lower legs

Pony: a horse that is at most 14.2 hands (58 inches/145 cm) tall at the withers

Shying: what it's called when a horse jumps away from something that frightens it; more commonly called "spooking"

Sire: the father of a horse

Stallion: a male horse four years old or older

Tack: the saddle, bridle, and other equipment worn by a riding horse

Weanling: a foal that is old enough to eat grass and no longer drinks its mother's milk

Withers: the bony bump in between the horse's back and its mane; it's the top of a horse's shoulder

Yearling: a one-year-old horse

Mix and Maxim!

A "maxim" is a saying that sums up a basic rule about how the world works. You've used maxims if you've ever said something like "an apple a day keeps the doctor away" or "you can't teach an old dog new tricks."

The horse, of course, has nuzzled its way into maxims, too. Here are a few that you're likely to hear, even from people who aren't horse crazy. See if you can match them up with their meanings! (Answers are upside down at the bottom of the page.)

1. You can lead a horse to water, but you can't make him drink.
2. Don't put the cart before the horse.
3. Don't switch horses in midstream.
4. That's a horse of a different color!
5. Don't lock the barn door after the horse has run away.
6. Don't look a gift horse in the mouth.
7. If wishes were horses, then beggars would ride.

a. It's better to prepare ahead of time instead of trying to fix things after the damage has been done.
b. Don't change your plans or your leader in the middle of doing something.
c. Don't pry and try to find out how much a present is worth—just accept it graciously.
d. That's something completely different.
e. Everybody could have what they want—if they could get it just by wishing for it!
f. You can show people how to do something, but you can't force them to do it that way.
g. Do things in the right order.

Answers: 1-f, 2-g, 3-b, 4-d, 5-a, 6-c, 7-e

A Horse by Any Other Name

Even in English, there's more than one way to say "horse." You can also call it one of the names listed below. Though you better think twice before using some of these terms to describe somebody *else's* horse—as you'll see, not all the names are flattering and many have faded from common use(*)!

Charger: A warhorse used for "charging," or running toward another army.*

Courser: A strong, fast horse.*

Dobbin: This word for "horse" may have sprung from its use as a common name for an individual horse more than 500 years ago, just as "Rover" has long been a favorite name for a dog.*

Gee-gee: This word comes from "baby talk" for "horse," and is likely based on the sound of a horse's whinny. (A horse is a *gee-gee* much like a dog is a *woof-woof* in baby talk!)*

Hack: "Hacking" is riding just for fun, so a "hack" is a riding horse. It was originally used to refer to horses that were hired out for riding. These poor horses wore out fast, so sometimes "hack" means a worn-out horse.

Hayburner: Any horse can be a hayburner because horses eat hay and "burn it" to make energy. This word is usually used just for fun, but it can also refer to a horse who doesn't work and just hangs around eating hay. A hayburner can also be called a haybag.

Mount: Getting on a horse is called "mounting," and so a horse is your "mount."

Nag: Long ago, as far back as the 1300s, this word referred to a pony. Nowadays, it means a broken-down horse.

Palfrey: a riding horse. This word was used in medieval times to describe a small, gentle horse ridden by a lady, as opposed to a big warhorse ridden by a knight.*

Plater: A word for "racehorse" that comes from Great Britain, where a "plate" is the trophy awarded to the winner of a horse race.

Plug: An old, worn-out horse, or a horse that moves slowly and unwillingly.

Steed: A horse, usually a stallion. In medieval times it meant "not a palfrey!" Nowadays, it's usually used in a funny way—like to call a Shetland pony a "noble steed."

What's What on a Horse

Here's a horse with all his body parts labeled. Most of these terms are used to describe parts on dogs and other animals, too.

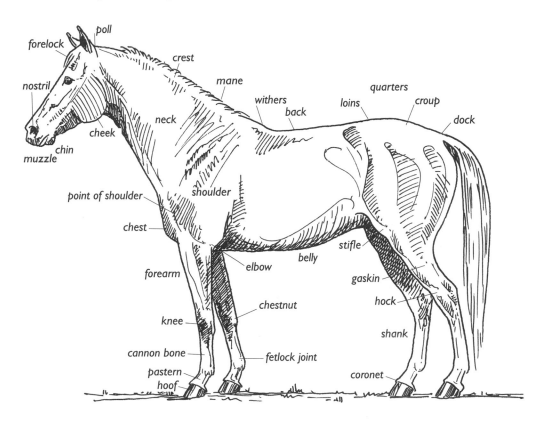

Give the Horse a Hand!

A horse's height is traditionally measured using a unit called a "hand." A hand is equal to 4 inches (10.2 cm). It's based on a "handy," old-time method of measuring a horse using the width of the palm of a man's hand. After all, a farmer might not carry a ruler around in case he needs to measure a horse—but he'd always have a hand! (It may sound funny, but it's no weirder than using a "foot" to measure height.)

Today, people use a measuring stick, not their hands, to measure a horse. The measurement tells how tall the horse is at the top of its withers. (That's a good place to measure because it stays put—unlike the head, which a horse is constantly raising and lowering.)

"Hands" is often shortened to "hh." So if you see that a horse is, say, "15.2 hh," 15 hands and 2 inches—that's 62 inches (5 feet, 2 inches—or in metric, 1.6 meters).

Just Say "Neigh"

Next time you're around a horse, take a good, hard look at it. Study it. Check out the way it places its legs and how it raises and lowers its neck. Focus on the way it swivels its ears and turns its head to look around. (It'll probably point its ears at you and study you, too!)

Horses, just like dogs and cats, use sounds and signals to show how they feel and to communicate with other horses—and people, too. It's up to us to learn how to "read" horses in order to understand them. Being able to understand "horse talk" helps you work with a horse, encourage it to do its best, and also become its friend.

Life in a Herd

To understand how a horse sees the world and how he communicates, it's important to remember that he's a prey animal (an animal hunted by predators) who's naturally inclined to live with other horses in a herd.

Being a prey animal that runs away from danger explains why a horse is so alert and why he can be so quick to shy, and bolt when startled.

That's why a horse may spook at the sight of an open umbrella or another harmless object. He just reacts reflexively, without even thinking, and skitters sideways or runs. After all, there's plenty of time to think about the harmlessness of umbrellas after you've run to safety—but if it were a cougar and you didn't scoot, you'd be lunch!

Living in a herd is also a good defense against predators. A horse in a herd benefits by having lots of eyes, ears, and other senses on the alert for danger in addition to his own.

In the wild, a horse herd, or "band," basically consists of a stallion, a few mares, and their young. The youngsters are foals born during the year as well as yearling colts and fillies. There may even be some two-year-olds still hanging around in the band.

Who's Who in the Herd

Most people think of the stallion as the big leader of the band—and he *does* have an important role to play: After all, he's the father of all the young 'uns, and he fights off other stallions who try to take over the band or steal his mares. This benefits the stallion because he doesn't want to lose his band, but it also benefits the mares because a new stallion might harm their foals since they don't belong to him.

But the day-to-day decision-maker in the band is a lead mare. She's the one whom the other mares acknowledge as "top dog." She's usually older and wiser, with lots of knowledge gleaned from a life of experience. She decides where the band should go to find food or water. She disciplines foals and yearlings with the help of other mares. When the band runs for danger, the lead mare is at the front, leading the charge, while the stallion brings up the rear to protect the band from behind.

Fillies and colts have a good time living in the band until they grow up. Then the stallion kicks them out! He drives them away by the time they are two to three years old. The fillies quickly join another stallion's band. The colts buddy up with other colts and stallions who don't have bands of their own. They form all-male groups called "bachelor bands."

Horses at a stable or on a farm don't live in a band like their wild cousins do—not even at a breeding stable. Stallions are often kept apart from other horses. Mares live with other mares and their foals. Geldings live with mares and other geldings. Nobody needs to run from danger. But each horse still needs to know the horses that share its world and how to get along with them.

Stable Relationships!

In real life, even though a wild mustang stallion's jobs keep him very busy, he's really content to just hang out with his friends, the mares, and graze. Stallions in the wild sometimes even play with foals.

Mares form strong friendships with each other, too. Foals make friends with other foals and play with them for many hours a day. Geldings also form friendships. In the past, when ranches released geldings used as cowhorses to roam the range in winter, groups of mares and geldings bunched together and hung out with each other—and the geldings frequently doted on the youngest in the bunch. (Cowboy author Will James spends many pages describing the fond attachments formed between geldings and their gentleness with foals in his book *Smoky*.)

Stable and farm horses form bonds, too. If you spend any time at a stable, you'll see that each horse has a buddy or two that he especially likes. These are pals he'd save seats for at lunchtime if horses ate in cafeterias! He may graze with his buddy, groom him, or just stand nose to tail with him, swishing tails and chasing away flies. If his pal's taken away to go on a trail ride or to join a riding lesson, he may whinny mournfully when he leaves—and joyfully when he returns.

There are also horses he won't care much about one way or another. And then, of course, there are horses he can't stand. Horses practically glare at stablemates whom they dislike (at our stable, this nasty look is called "stink-eye"). They pin back their ears if they get close to each other. Sometimes they nip or kick.

EACH HORSE IS UNIQUE

This just in! Scientists have recently confirmed what horses have known forever: Every horse has its own particular whinny, and other horses who hear it know who's neighing, even if they can't see the horse.

But most of the time, the horses just want life to be easygoing. They don't spend all their time vying to be top horse or putting other horses in their place. There are squabbles now and then, but for the most part, the horses get along—especially if their owner's been smart enough not to put "mortal enemies" in the same paddock!

Neighs and Nickers

Horses evolved to live in close-knit bands in wide-open spaces. They didn't have to shout at other horses to keep in touch because they were close together, without any trees and leaves to block their views of each other. That's why horses mainly communicate with body language. They say a lot just by how they stand, walk, or move their ears.

But because humans are a chatty species and like to talk, talk, talk (do you know where your cell phone is?), we'll start with the sounds that horses make.

Neigh: Everybody knows a horse says "neigh"! It's a sound right up there alongside the well-known "moo," "meow," and "cluck." A horse neighs to keep in touch with a horse that's far away, especially if he can't see the other horse. It's a loud sound that travels far. A horse may also neigh when he sees his owner. Mares and foals neigh to each other, too. A neigh is also known as a "whinny."

Nicker: This is that nice, rumbling sound a horse sometimes makes when you approach him. It's basically "hello"—a friendly sound. A horse may also nicker to tell another horse he means no harm. Mares nicker to their foals. Horses may nicker at humans not only to greet them but also to suggest that an apple would be appreciated.

Blow: This is a huff of air pushed out of the nostrils. A short, sharp blow is an alarm. It puts other horses on alert, too. Longer blows are more like sighs.

Snort: A snort is just what it sounds like—a loud snort! A horse snorts by quickly forcing air out of his nose. It's a loud blow with a fluttery, rippling sound added to it. Snorting may mean a horse is excited or restless. But sometimes a snort just means a horse has dust or a fly in his nose!

Squeal: This is the high-pitched sound you'll hear from a horse when he's telling another horse to keep away—it's kind of like saying, "Hey, quit it!" Foals also squeal when they play.

Roar and bellow: Let's hope you never hear a horse you ride roar and bellow! These sounds are made by really angry horses—usually fighting stallions.

As you can see, the list of sounds horses make is pretty short. Horses mainly use their ears, facial expressions, and body language to communicate.

The Ears Have It

ears pricked forward

A horse can turn his ears in all directions as he listens to sounds. You can often tell what a horse is paying attention to by looking at where his ears are pointing.

A horse's ears are also a clue to his feelings. If his ears are pricked—facing forward—he's interested and alert. It's nice to see ears like that if you're approaching a horse to pet it or ride it. He may also be moving his ears all over the place—even in different directions. In that case, he's probably just taking in lots of sounds as well as your approach. If he's got "airplane ears"—ears sticking out sideways—he may be relaxed, tired, or feeling down.

airplane ears

The ears you want to beware of are ears that are flipped back. Ears pointing backward indicate a horse who's listening to something behind him—or a horse who's a little cross. And you really want to stay away if those ears are pinned back hard,

ears flipped back

flat against his head. This signals that the horse is very angry. You might get hurt if you get any closer. They clearly warn, "Stay away!"

Heads Up!

Ever notice how a horse usually lifts her head when you approach? She does this partly to get a good look at you. She's also doing this because she looks larger and more dominant this way. (She's not *thinking* that—it just comes naturally to her.) A horse that's scared or excited lifts its head high, too. A stallion showing off in front of a mare or another stallion holds his head high while arching his neck.

A relaxed horse holds its head more or less in line with her body and just "looks" at ease all over. But a tense horse with her neck held stiff and low is being aggressive. (A wild stallion herds his mares or chases away other males by "snaking" his neck this way and using his teeth.)

arching neck

This "snaky" neck and head looks different from the stretched neck and head of a submissive horse—one that's saying "you're the boss." Foals and young horses often stretch this way while "chewing" the air in front of them. They're not trying to bite! This motion is called "mouthing," "snapping," or "champing," and it means "I'm no threat—don't hurt me." It's a little like the gesture of a submissive dog who ducks her head and approaches you meekly, licking her own nose.

Tell-Tails!

A horse's tail is more than just a pretty waterfall of hair or a well-placed flyswatter. It can also express a horse's feelings.

A horse who holds his tail up high and swishes it may simply be feeling his oats—life is good and he's full of energy. Foals often hold their fluffy tails high as they play.

A tail held high and stiffly, however, may be a sign that the horse is agitated. A stallion, for example, holds his tail up if he's prancing and showing off for a mare, but also if he's challenging another stallion.

Like an angry cat lashing its tail, a horse who switches his tail sharply is in a bad mood. Something's bugging him—and although it may be just a fly, it could be the person riding him.

A horse with his tail clamped tightly to his hind end is a worried, fearful horse. He may simply be showing submission and telling another horse that he's no threat. He may be feeling threatened and getting ready to kick, if his tightly tucked tail pairs up with a rounded rump or a lifted hind leg. Or he may just be feeling unwell. You can't always be sure, but most of the time it's clear that you should probably be extra careful around him.

In short, tail talk just makes sense: A horse with a fidgety tail is in a snit, and a content horse has a relaxed tail that flicks now and then to brush away a fly.

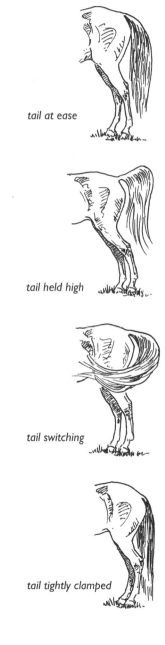

tail at ease

tail held high

tail switching

tail tightly clamped

A Leg Up

Have you ever watched a horse just hanging out in a paddock or tied to a post? Sometimes, such a horse will be so relaxed that she's dozed off. Or she might bear her weight on three legs, with one hind leg resting so that just the tip of her hoof is touching the ground.

You've probably also seen horses pawing at the ground with a front leg. A horse may do this if he's feeling impatient or frustrated. He's acting a little like a person anxiously tapping a pencil on a desk or a foot on the floor. Horses also paw to uncover food that's covered with snow or straw, or to rough up a place where they're thinking of rolling.

pawing

You may have also seen horses stamping their hooves. A horse may stamp to get rid of a fly. A stamp of a front hoof can also be a warning, a sign that a horse is irritated by or impatient with the person saddling him. A horse may also stamp to warn another horse that he's getting annoyed.

Horses strike out with their forelegs at horses who annoy them. They also strike out with their forelegs and kick with their hind legs when they play. You don't want to get involved with this kind of horseplay—a playful kick is all in fun to a horse, but can injure or kill a human.

striking

A kick from a hind leg is powerful and hard, and horse people do everything they can to avoid such a kick. They don't surprise a horse by coming up or crossing behind him without any warning. When they work with a horse, they stay out of the path of

kicking from the hind legs

a kick. They also watch the horse's body language.

A frightened horse who might suddenly kick shows he's scared by raising his head and clamping down his tail. His eyes are wide, his nostrils flared. A horse may also kick because he's an aggressive sort. He'll hump up his back and turn his tail toward you. A horse, before kicking, may also just lift a hind hoof and wave it around.

Or he may give no warning at all. It's always important to wear a helmet, steer clear of the hind end, and watch carefully when you work with a horse.

Red Ribbon = DANGER!

You should be careful around any horse—but be extra careful if a horse has a red ribbon tied in his tail. It means he's a kicker. A rider with a horse who kicks ties a red ribbon on the horse's tail to warn other riders to be extra careful around him and to keep their horses away.

Sophie Says: Kvik is a Fjord pony that I ride a lot. But Kvik kicks! He's nice, but he's very touchy with his hind feet. When you reach down to pick up the foot you want, he'll slash it out sideways. Then he'll pull it back, looking innocent. You basically have to sing to him to make him hold his feet still for you!

Cow-Like

A horse can kick like a cow! A "cow kick" is a kick forward with a hind leg. A horse may cow-kick to get a fly off her belly. She may also cow-kick if she's cross with you or because you hit a ticklish spot while grooming her.

A Horse from Head to Hoof

A horse is an amazing animal that is a blend of human tinkering and wild nature. Thousands of years of breeding have produced horses that excel at jobs people want them to do. By picking and choosing certain types of stallions and mares to mate, people have created an incredible variety: long-limbed horses that run fast, powerful horses that jump, sturdy ponies that can safely carry the smallest riders, even horses that move in special ways.

Horses Big and Small

One result of specialized breeding is the enormous range in sizes of modern horses. Some horses are taller at the shoulder than a basketball player, while others are barely bigger than a German shepherd!

Higher Shires and Mini Whinnies!

For height, you really have to "hand" it to the Shire! This draft horse is the tallest breed. A typical Shire may be 17 hands high. The tallest horse ever measured was a Shire named Sampson, who was born in England in 1846. He measured 21.25 hands high.

On the other end of the scale are miniature horses, such as the American Miniature and the Falabella. These little horses are so small, they're not even measured in hands—or at the withers! Their height is measured from the last hairs in the mane, in inches. An American Miniature, for example, measures no more than 34 inches (86 cm) tall. The smallest horse ever was a Falabella named Little Pumpkin, who was born in 1973. He was a mere 14 inches tall.

The smallest full-grown horse alive today is Thumbelina, an American Miniature who is only 17 ½ inches (44.5 cm) tall. When she stands next to a regular-sized horse, she's barely tall enough to nuzzle its knee! She is extra small because she was born with a condition called "dwarfism." The little horse suffered some health problems at first but overcame them. Today she is a "spokes-horse" who goes on tour to raise money to benefit children's hospitals and other places that help kids.

Heavy as a Horse

Thumbelina weighs a mere 57 pounds (26 kg)—less than most full-grown Labrador retrievers. A horse you ride at a stable weighs a lot more! A typical riding horse usually weighs between 800 to 1,200 pounds (363 to 544 kg). A big draft horse, however, can weigh 1,500 pounds (680 kg) or more.

How do you weigh a horse? There are horse scales that are basically super-sized versions of the scales used to weigh dogs at a vet's office. But horse people can also estimate a horse's weight by measuring parts of its body with a tape measure. Here's how:

First, you take two measurements, in either inches or centimeters: the "heartgirth" and "body length." Heartgirth is the measurement around the horse's body. "Body length" is how long he is from the point of his shoulder to his backside.

Then you plug the numbers into this formula (if you're using inches):

[(Heartgirth x Heartgirth) x Body Length] ÷ 330* = Weight (lbs)

Let's take, as an example, a horse whose heartgirth measures 70 inches and who is 72 inches long. Here's the formula in steps to show how it works (rounding off the answer):

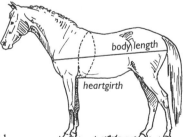

   a. 70 x 70 = 4,900
   b. 4,900 x 72 = 352,800
   c. 352,800 ÷ 330 = 1,069 pounds

But if you don't feel like doing all this math, you can use a height/weight tape. It's a measuring tape with estimated weights printed on it that you wrap around the horse's girth.

*(If you use centimeters, divide by 11,877 instead of 330. Your answer will be the horse's weight in kilograms.)

when is a horse a pony?

A pony is a horse that measures no more than 14.2 hands high. But height is not the only thing that makes a horse a pony. A pony's body is usually longer than its height, while a horse's body length and height are about the same. The pony's body is usually thicker for its size than a horse's body, too. And a pony usually has a thicker coat than a horse, as well as a thicker mane and tail. Many ponies also have broader, shorter heads than other horses.

OLDEST HORSE EVER

The longest-living horse on record was an English workhorse named Old Billy. He was foaled in 1760 and lived to the ripe old age of sixty-two, according to the *Guinness Book of World Records*. He pulled barges right up until he was fifty-nine!

Ha-ha! Horse Laughs

Why did the pony cough a lot?
Because he was a little hoarse.

Why did the foal wear a blanket?
Because he was a little colt.

How long should a horse's legs be?
Long enough to reach the ground!

What do you call a fake horse?
A phony pony.

Why do horses make such good friends?
Because you can have stable relationships with them.

Why is a stable like a wedding?
Because it's got bridles and grooms.

What did the clueless new rider say when she was put on a Quarter Horse?
"He's only a quarter horse? Sure looks like he's all horse to me!"

What has four legs and flies?
A horse.

Horse Sense

No matter what breed a horse is, he has built-in knowledge inherited from his ancestors, who had to watch out for danger and run for their lives. This built-in knowledge is called "instinct." Those instincts are aided by sharp senses of sight, hearing, and smell, which keep the horse informed about everything happening around him.

On the Watch

Not much gets by a horse. Its whole head is built so that it doesn't miss a thing.

For starters, a horse has a long face. Being "horse-faced" means a horse can safely lower its head to graze because its eyes can still see over the grass and watch for danger. Its eyes are like those of other prey animals. They are on the sides of the head, facing slightly forward, enabling the horse to see nearly all around it without even turning its head.

A horse does have some blind spots, however. It can't see what's right in front of its face and under its nose, and it can't see things directly behind its head and past its tail. That's why your fingers might get nipped if you don't hold your hand flat when you give a horse a treat—it can't see what's in your hand and just uses its muzzle and teeth to nab the food. And that's also why you have to let a horse know you're behind it and not just sneak up without warning!

Hang out around horses long enough, and you'll see that horse people talk to horses when they approach them. Many a rider who needs to cross behind a horse lays a hand on the horse's rump first. Then she slides her hand across the rump as she moves from one side of the horse to the other. That way, the horse can figure out where the rider is by the touch of her hand and won't be startled or inclined to kick.

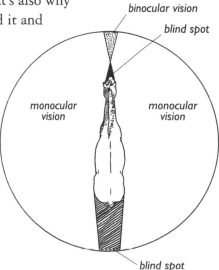

Seeing in 3-D

The back of a horse's eye has a long, thin, extra-sensitive strip in it—perfect for scanning the horizon for danger on either side. But a horse can also see in 3-D like you can. This 3-D area, where the sights seen by both his left and right eye overlap, is in front of the horse. Seeing in 3-D helps a horse judge depth and distance. A horse uses his 3-D, or "binocular," vision to figure out how deep a hole is or how tall and far away a jump is.

A horse moves his head to bring his binocular vision into the right spot to see things clearly. To focus on something close to him, a horse arches his neck and tucks in his chin to

---

Look Before You Leap!

A horse can't see a jump as she leaps over it! It disappears from her sight when she lifts the front of her body to take the jump. She has to use her memory of the jump as she saw it on the approach when she soars over it.

---

peer at it. He holds his head at about a 45-degree angle to study something in the distance. He drops his head to look at something on the ground in front of his feet.

When he's not using his binocular vision, each of his eyes is taking in a different view. A horse can see what's in front with one eye while looking backward with the other eye! This kind of vision is called "monocular," or "one eye," vision. It's not great for judging depth and distance, but it's perfect for seeing motion and detecting predators.

Blind Spots

You're nearly invisible to your horse when you're sitting on her back! That's because you're sitting in one of her blind spots. If you can't see either one of her eyes, she can't see you. But she can easily peek at you by turning her head slightly.

In Not-So-Living Color

A horse doesn't see as many colors as you do. His world is mostly made up of grays, blues, and yellows. A red apple looks sort of grayish yellow to him, with maybe a tint of blue. Green grass is yellow gray in his eyes. Your hot-pink half-chaps are boringly gray.

Listen Up!

A horse not only sees differently from a human—he also hears differently. He can hear some high-pitched sounds that you can't. He can also pick up sounds too low or far away for you to hear.

A horse fine-tunes his hearing by swiveling his ears in all directions. He can point both ears to the source of a sound to listen to it more closely. He can flip his ears back to listen to his rider's voice. A horse may even flip one ear back to hear his rider and point the other one forward!

Some horses are spooked by sudden or loud sounds. These horses' riders may tuck cotton wool or special pom-pom earplugs into their mounts' ears to dampen sound and help keep them calm.

Eerie Ears!

The Kathiawari and the Marwari are two breeds from India that are famous for their ears, which are long and curve inward so that the tips touch.

breezy = uneasy

Why do some horses freak out on windy days? Many horse people think it's because the wind makes it hard for a horse to pinpoint the sources of sounds. This makes a horse nervous.

Horse Scents

Horses smell a lot better than people do.
(No, not *that* kind of smell—in this case,
it's about their *ability* to smell!) A
horse's nose is much more sensitive
than yours is. Compared to horses,
we humans are walking around with
clothespins stuck on our noses, our
nostrils clamped shut!

A horse easily picks up smells from a
distance of about 600 feet (180 m). On a breezy day, he
may be able to sniff out a strong scent that's a mile (1.6 km) away. He can
flare his nostrils wide to take in even more air. Once the air is inside his
nose, it swirls through a maze of bones lined with scent-sensitive cells.

Some extra-interesting smells make a horse flip up his upper lip so that
he looks like he's laughing. What he's really doing is letting the smell drift
over a part of his nose called the Jacobson's organ. This sensitive body part
studies the smell even more intently—kind of like a nosy version of a
magnifying glass! A male horse often does this if he smells a mare.

A horse also uses its keen sense of smell to identify other horses and to
tell friends and strangers apart. Smell, too, is an important part of the
bonding that happens when a mare sniffs at her newborn foal. Horses also
pick up important info about other horses in the area by smelling their
droppings, just as dogs and many other animals do.

Horsey Touch and Taste

Just as important as smell is a horse's sense of touch. A horse's skin is so
sensitive that she can feel a tiny fly land on it. Muscles under the skin
twitch to flick the annoying pest away. Most sensitive of all is the muzzle.
Its soft, velvety skin and fringe of whiskers help the horse feel things
that she can't clearly see. The lips work like fingers to
manipulate items (including locks on stall doors!).

Those lips can also deftly pluck
bits of apple, grapes, and
carrot off the palm
of your hand.

A horse's sense of taste is much like yours. It can detect salty, sour, bitter, and sweet flavors—with "sweet" being its favorite! Sugary, sweet molasses is sometimes added to horse feed to get a picky eater to chow down.

Favorite Horse Foods

Horses mainly eat grass, hay, and oats. They also like snacks.

Sugar cubes were once a common treat, but now people tend to give horses more healthful snacks, such as bits of carrot and apple. Many horses also love to eat peppermints! (Peppermints aren't any more healthful than a sugar cube, but at least they won't crumble to bits in your pocket as sugar cubes do.)

Horses also have individual tastes, just as people do. Horses in the Middle East are often fed dates as snacks. Australian horses nibble on sunflower seeds. And horses in Iceland readily eat salted herring— a fish dish!

Got Treats?

Do you like snacks? Horses sure do. These easy-to-make cookies include some of a horse's favorite foods. They're a great gift for a favorite horse.

Pony Cakes
1 cup rolled oats
1 cup flour
1 tsp salt
2 tsp sugar
2 tsp corn oil
¼ cup molasses
1 cup shredded carrots
1 cup diced apple

1. Preheat the oven to 350°F (177°C).*
2. Mix the oats, flour, salt, sugar, oil, and molasses in a bowl.
3. Stir in the carrots and apple.
4. Lightly flour your hands to keep the batter from sticking to them. Then form balls of batter no bigger than a golf ball.
5. Grease a cookie sheet (rub it with butter or margarine or spritz it with a spray-on cooking oil).
6. Place the balls of batter on the cookie sheet.
7. Bake for about 12 minutes or until the cookies turn gold.
8. Let cool.
9. Serve to your favorite horse.

*Ask an adult to help you with tasks involving the oven.

The Horse's Mouth

A horse's teeth are built to chew grass. Grass contains a tough, sandlike substance called silica. Silica is hard on teeth because it wears them down, as if the horse were eating sandpaper! So an animal that feeds on grass needs tough, long teeth.

A horse's tooth is certainly tough enough. One of its outer layers is made of enamel, a substance that's stronger than bone. (Your teeth have enamel, too.)

A HORSE'S TEETH

An adult female horse has thirty-six teeth. An adult male has forty teeth. His extra teeth consist of four small canines, which are often called tushes or tusks. Sometimes, a mare may have them, too. Some horses also grow four extra teeth called "wolf teeth." They get in the way of the bit, so they are usually removed.

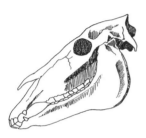

Unlike your teeth, however, a horse's choppers keep pushing up out of its jaws during its life.

Sometimes you'll hear people say that the horse's teeth grow throughout its life. Actually, they grow early in the horse's life and then just take their time showing up in its mouth!

What happens when a horse gets old and its teeth are worn down to stubs? In the wild, such an old horse would starve to death—if it wasn't caught by a predator first. Domestic senior-citizen horses, however, are fed mushy, soft food that they don't need to chew so much.

Open Wide!

An expert horseperson, such as a vet or a breeder, can figure out how old a horse is by looking at its teeth. A horse's teeth grow, change, and wear out over the course of its life. An examination of the teeth can give a rough idea of the horse's age.

teeth of a six-year-old horse

Baby Horse Teeth

A foal has "milk" or baby teeth. Her twenty-four baby teeth are all in place by the time she's nine months old. She won't have her full mouth of grown-up teeth until she's about five years old. Sadly, she doesn't have a pillow to place the baby teeth under for a tooth fairy to find!

Eating Like a Horse

A horse's digestive system is built for eating small meals over many hours. That's why a horse "eats like a horse"—almost constantly!

The horse's rubbery lips gather up food. Sharp front teeth nip off blades of grass. A space in between the front teeth and the back teeth makes a great pocket for holding food briefly. (It's also turned out to be a handy place to put a bit.)

The back teeth grind the food and mix it with saliva to make it easier to swallow. A horse makes about 10 gallons (38 liters) of saliva a day. Just picture ten of those big plastic one-gallon milk jugs lined up, and you'll see how much spit that is!

Then *gulp*, down it all goes into the horse's throat, or esophagus. A horse's esophagus is about 4.5 feet long (1.4 m)—about five times as long as a person's!

The esophagus leads into the stomach. A horse's stomach is much like yours, except that it holds a lot more food! Your stomach can hold a bit more than a quart (.9 liters) of food—and even more if you really stuff yourself (stomachs are stretchy). A horse's stomach can hold nearly 5 gallons (19 liters) of food.

That sounds like a lot, but it's really not much for an animal as big as a horse. A cow, for example, can hold about 50 gallons (190 liters) in its four-chambered stomach—that's ten times more than a horse can!

Ew . . . Slobber!

Have you ever seen a horse whose mouth is bubbling with foam? Maybe you've even had a horse rub its muzzle on your shirt, using you as a human napkin to wipe off drool! Just what is this foamy stuff, and why do horses "froth at the mouth," anyway?

The froth is simply saliva that gets bubbly when it's mixed up with air. The horse makes the saliva foamy when it plays with the bit in its mouth by chewing it lightly and moving its tongue. He may also lick his lips.

Many riders and trainers actually consider some froth to be a good thing. It can be a sign that the horse is enjoying his work, paying attention, and "accepting" the bit in his mouth. If he's happy in his work, he's also relaxed. This makes his jaw muscles relaxed, too, and encourages him to champ and chew.

There's also a kind of fungus that sometimes grows on clover in a pasture. A horse that eats it doesn't get sick, but it makes him produce oceans of slobber. Yuck!

Intestine Digestion

The horse's stomach breaks down food, but it doesn't soak up nutrition from it. That job is left to the horse's small intestine. "Small" is kind of a funny word to describe this body part, because the horse's "small" intestine is actually about 70 feet (21 m) long. That's nearly the length of two school buses! (It fits inside the horse because it's all coiled up.)

Digestive fluids in the small intestine break down the food even more so the horse's body can absorb nutrition from it. But wait! There's more! Yep—about 29 feet (8.8 m) more. That's how long the next part of the horse's digestive system is. This part is the large intestine.

First stop in the large intestine is a pouch that's about 4 feet (1.2 m) long, called the cecum. It can hold more than twice as much food as the stomach can. It's basically a big vat full of one-celled creatures called microbes.

Without a bellyful of microbes, a horse couldn't digest the bulk of what it eats. It's these itty-bitty microbes that break down the tough walls of plant cells in food like grass and hay.

Food spends about seven hours stewing in the cecum before moving on to the rest of the large intestine. There, more microbes wait for their chance to attack the food. They may work on it for the next two or three days.

Finally, what doesn't get digested exits the horse at the tail end. A typical horse produces about 50 pounds (23 kg) of manure each day. That adds up to about 9 tons a year—enough to fill a city garbage truck. No wonder horse girls spend so much time mucking out stalls!

URP!

You'll probably never have to scold a horse for rudely burping. Most horses can't burp! They can't throw up, either.

At first, this sounds okay—throwing up is gross, right? But it actually serves a useful purpose. Throwing up food that may be poisonous is definitely a good thing. A horse that has eaten too much and feels lots of pressure in its stomach would also benefit by being able to throw up.

Horses actually pay a high price for the privilege of not throwing up. That "price" is a condition called colic.

"Colic" is a word used by horse people to describe problems with a horse's digestive system. A horse with colic feels pain in its abdomen. It may kick and bite at its sides, lie down and roll, stamp its feet, and groan as it tries to relieve the pain. The cause of the pain may be a simple tummy-ache—but it can also be caused by something very serious, such as a twisted intestine.

Colic can be a life-or-death situation for a horse, so horse owners are quick to call the vet if simple remedies fail to relieve the horse's pain.

WHEN IS A **Burp** NOT A BURP?

Though most horses can't burp, some owners report that they've heard theirs belch. One horse owner described her horse's belching to a vet because she worried it was a problem. But apparently it wasn't. Her vet just told her to enjoy her "weird, happy, healthy, burping horse."

Ha-ha! Horse Laughs

Why did the mare get a scolding?
Because she was trying to stirrup trouble.

What's a horse's favorite sport?
Stable tennis!

What do you call a spotted horse that never wins a race?
An Appa-loser.

What do you get when a wild horse turns into a car?
A mustang convertible.

What did the Hanoverian do when he won first place in the hunter event?
He jumped for joy!

What hair style do Shetlands always wear?
Pony tails!

How is a bridle like a week of wet weather?
One has reins and the other has rains.

Drink Up!

A horse drinks up to 8 gallons (32 liters) of water a day. That's about two big buckets of water. He may need even more if he's working hard or the weather is hot. A horse drinks water by sucking it up. He doesn't lap it up with his tongue like a cat or dog does.

Take a Deep Breath!

A horse's breathing system works the same way yours does—but, of course, everything is bigger in the horse. And you can't flare your nostrils the way he can!

At rest, a horse takes about eight to fourteen breaths per minute. (An adult human takes about 12 to 20 breaths per minute, a child about 16 to 25.) The air is warmed as it flows through the horse's long nose. Fine hairs in the nose filter out dust.

A hard-working horse, however, breathes faster, just as you do when you run. A racehorse, for example, may take about 120 breaths per minute as it gallops down the home stretch.

As you might guess, a horse's heart pumps faster when it exercises, too, just as yours does. At rest, a horse's heart beats about 36 to 42 times a minute. That rate increases to as much as 240 beats per minute for that horse running across the finish line.

A big animal like a horse needs a big heart to pump blood throughout its body. Your heart is about the size of your clenched fist—but a horse's is about the size of a basketball! The average horse's heart weighs from 8 to 10 pounds (4 to 5 kg). But some top racehorses have extra-large hearts that weigh from 14 to 20 pounds (10 kg).

ALL HEART

The famous racehorse Secretariat had a heart about three times bigger than the average horse. Its weight was estimated at about 22 pounds (10 kg). Horse experts think his big heart was one reason for Secretariat's incredible racing power.

By a Nose

A horse can't breathe through his mouth. He can only breathe through his nostrils. That's because his airway is separated from his mouth by a flap that opens up only when he swallows. This flap keeps him from breathing in bits of food and choking on it. Because a horse can't breathe through his mouth, he can't pant like a dog to cool off.

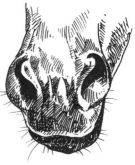

Huffing and Puffing

You can tell when a horse is breathing in and when she's breathing out just by watching her run. That's because her breathing is linked to her hoof beats when she canters or gallops.

The horse breathes out when her front hooves touch the ground and her neck and head are thrust down and forward. She breathes in while she's suspended in the air, getting ready to take her next stride with her head held up.

And here's a fun fact to surprise a horse-crazy friend with: A horse holds its breath when it goes over a jump. It breathes out when it lands and breathes normally again until its next jump.

Horses Hot and Cold

You may see horses described as being hot-blooded, cold-blooded, or warm-blooded. These terms don't actually mean the temperature of its blood—all horses are warm-blooded. They describe *types* of horses.

"Hot bloods" are speedy, energetic sorts of horses, like Thoroughbreds and Arabians. "Cold bloods" are strong, calm, steady horses, like Shires and Clydesdales. "Warm bloods" are a mix, like Quarter Horses and Irish Hunters. Any of these horses will have a body temperature that's about 101.5°F (38°C).

Happy Birthday, Horses!

Start your year off right by singing "Happy Birthday, Horses" on January 1. The first of January is the official birthday of all Thoroughbred racehorses born in the United States, Canada, and other countries north of the equator during the previous year. Sing again on August 1, and you'll be sending happy-birthday greetings to many horses in Australia and other places south of the equator where August 1 is an official equine birth date.

Horsey Legs and feet

"No foot, no horse" is an old saying among horse people. It means that without a good set of feet and legs, a horse isn't much good to itself or to anybody else. Sounds harsh, but it's true that a horse depends on its limbs not only for getting around, but also for its all-around health.

Fleet Feet

Plenty of animals have four legs. But few of them can run as fast as a horse. A horse's legs are extra long for its body size. It covers lots of ground with every stride. This length is one reason why a horse can run faster and farther than other four-legged animals.

All that pounding-hoofbeats stuff puts a lot of pressure on a horse's limbs, but its bones are built to endure it. Its hooves are, too. A horse's foot contains fatty pads that work like shock absorbers. Other parts of the foot flex and stretch to help spread out the force of the hoof hitting the ground.

Got a Nail File?

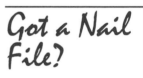

A horse's hoof grows nearly half an inch (1.2 cm) a month. Your fingernails take about three months to grow that much.

Asleep on Its Feet

How can a horse sleep standing up? It doesn't sound restful, but for a horse, it's easy. His legs contain a system of bones, muscles, and tough elastic cords that lock in place to hold him up as he snoozes.

Have you ever seen a horse resting with one back leg relaxed, so that just the tip of his hoof touches the ground? This is another built-in sleep system at work. To use it, the horse rests one hind leg and leans most of his weight on the other. The horse shifts its weight from one leg to the other to give each one a rest.

Sleeping standing up is useful for an animal that might need to wake up quickly and run from an enemy. So it's natural for a horse to sleep standing up, and he can get much of the sleep he needs this way. But he must sometimes lie down to get extra deep sleep. A horse sleeping flat on its side also gets a chance to dream. He may even whinny in his sleep! Foals often sleep lying down because their moms are watching out for their safety.

Go, Horse, Go!

A horse's legs move in different patterns called "gaits." The four basic gaits are the walk, trot, canter, and gallop.

When your riding teacher sings out, "Walk on!" your horse steps out in a four-beat gait. First the legs on one side take turns moving forward, then the legs on the other side move. The horse always has three feet on the ground and just one off it. This gait makes the famous "clippety-clop" sound we associate with horses.

Walk

Need to speed up? Then it's time to move into a trot. The trot is a two-beat gait. (Think "trit-trot, trit-trot.") When she's trotting, a horse has only two feet on the ground at the same time. The legs move forward in diagonal pairs—front left with rear right, front right with rear left. In between beats, she's got all four feet off the ground for that split second.

Trot

The trot feels really bumpy to many new riders. So a rider needs to learn how to ride at the trot. English riders often "post," which means to alternately rise and sit in the saddle in sync with the horse's motion. Posting is also called "rising to the trot." This makes trotting more comfortable for horse and rider.

Canter

Head First

A lying-down horse always gets up by lifting the front of her body first, then the hind end. It's the opposite for a cow.

Traditionally, Western riders have used the "sitting trot," in which the rider sits deep in the saddle and relaxes into the rhythm of the trot so that any bounciness is absorbed by the rider's body. English riders also need to know how to "sit" a trot. Skill and practice make the trot comfortable for both horse and rider. No horse wants its rider to be skidding around in the saddle or banging up and down on its back!

Gallop

Flip book starts here and goes through page 71.

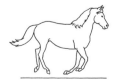

Flying Horses

From a trot, a horse moves into a three-beat gait called the canter. In this gait, a rear hoof hits the ground—*thump*! Then the other rear hoof and the front hoof that's diagonally opposite it hit the ground—*thump*! Finally, the other front hoof hits the ground—*thump*!

The front hoof that hits the ground last is called the "leading leg." If a horse is cantering and ends each stride with, say, his left leg, he's on the "left lead."

Speed up a canter and you get a gallop! That's the gait racehorses use. A gallop is a four-beat gait. Each hoof takes a turn hitting the ground. If the left rear hoof lands first, the next hoof will be the right rear, then the left front, then the right front— kind of a zigzag pattern. Then all four legs are quickly gathered under its body while the horse hurtles forward. All four feet are off the ground during this fraction of a second.

At a full gallop, a racehorse can take about two strides in just one second. One stride covers about 20 feet (6 m) of ground.

Sophie Says: My favorite gait is the canter. It's a smooth and rocking gait. You can watch everything going by really fast. It's a million times better than riding in a car.

Walk On By

Horses boast a few other gaits, most of which are linked to certain breeds. Many Standardbred racers *pace* instead of trot. A pacing horse moves both left legs forward at the same time, then both right legs.

American Saddlebreds are famous for a movement called the *slow gait*. It's a four-beat gait, with each hoof landing separately. The horse picks his knees up high with each step. The horse is trained to perform this gait—he isn't born with this ability.

Many Saddlebreds are also trained to perform the *rack*, which is like the slow gait but much faster. If you've ever seen a horse prance, you've got an idea of how these horses move!

Icelandic horses also do the rack, which is called the *tölt* in Iceland. Riders use the tölt to cross rugged, rocky land in this breed's homeland. Icelandic horses are not trained to tölt. This gait comes naturally to them.

Covering ground also led to the development of a breed called the Tennessee Walking Horse. Tennessee Walkers boast gliding, four-beat gaits called the *flat walk* and the *running walk*.

The *foxtrot* is another gait that got its start as a way to travel far over rough ground. It's the specialty of the Missouri Foxtrotter. A foxtrotting horse is often described as walking in front while trotting in back.

English and Western Riding Gaits?

Being a horse girl, you know there are two main styles of riding: English and Western. There are many differences between the two, but the main feature you'll notice is the distinctive saddle used in each discipline.

A Western saddle is big, with a deep seat and a horn. It was made for riding trails for hours on end and for use in roping cows. An English saddle is smaller and lacks a horn. It has its roots in Europe, where riders traveled long distances across countryside and jumped over obstacles along the way. They didn't need a horn, since they weren't roping cattle, and certainly didn't want a horn jabbing them in the stomach when they jumped!

Whether it's being ridden English-style or Western-style, a horse uses the same gaits. But riders use different words for them. If you're riding Western, you'd say "jog" and "lope" instead of "trot" and "canter"!

THE HIP BONE'S CONNECTED TO THE . . .

Want to know more about how a horse's body works? Check out the twelve-part series about horse anatomy produced by the magazine *The Horse*. Find it online at: www.thehorse.com/ ViewArticle.aspx?ID =9421

ZOOM!

How fast can a horse run? A typical riding horse can gallop at about 30 miles (48.3 km) per hour. A racehorse can reach speeds of about 40 miles (64.4 km) per hour, faster than the speed limit on town roads. But not as fast as a car on a highway!

Cool It!

Any horse that gets heated up while working needs to be cooled down after its work is done. Cooling down a horse involves walking it slowly until its body returns to a normal temperature. In hot weather, the horse may also be washed with cool water. In chilly weather, it may wear a blanket called a "cooler" while being walked.

Cooling down is important because a horse will get sick if it's allowed to stay over-heated or if it's chilled.

in a lather

Just like you, a horse sweats to cool off when it's hot. But because it's so big, it produces a lot more sweat than you do! A horse who's really working hard produces 3 to 4 gallons (10 to 15 liters) of sweat per hour. That's about three times as much as you'd perspire.

You may have also seen what looks like white soap scum on a sweaty horse's hide. This soapy-looking stuff is called "lather."

If you watch a horse race on TV, you may notice lather forming mainly on a horse's neck and the insides of its thighs. Lathering is normal, but if a horse gets really sweaty before the race even begins, it may be because he's really nervous or overexcited. If you're at the track, you'd say this horse is "washy."

A horse "lathers up" like this because his sweat is different from yours. It contains a substance called "latherin." Latherin makes the sweat sticky and helps it wet the horse's hairs so he can cool off.

TOP TEN WEIRD HORSE-AILMENT NAMES

Diseases and injuries aren't funny—but some of their names sure are.

Bog spavin—squishy swelling on a horse's hock
Bots—larvae of bot fly, which grow inside a horse after it licks fly eggs off its coat and cause stomach problems
Heaves—lung problem that makes it hard for a horse to breathe
Megrims—old name for dizzy spells in horses
Nasal gleet—runny nose
Poll-evil—injury on a horse's head behind the ears
Rainrot—crud on horse's skin caused by fungus
Seedy toe—separation of layers in a horse's hoof that causes a gap to grow
Stringhalt—jerking of a horse's hind legs when walking or trotting
Thumps—twitching of muscles in a horse's sides caused by overwork

A Horse of a Different Color: Coats, Manes, and Tails

Blacks and bays, dapples and grays—horses come in a rainbow of colors. Not only do they range from white to black and everything in between, they also bear markings on different parts of their bodies.

And as if this color-fest isn't enough, horse people seem to use two names for every single trait! A horse may be called "chestnut" in the eastern United States, for example, but "sorrel" on the West Coast.

Scientists and horse breeders have puzzled over horse color for many years. They've tried to figure out how horses pass along colors to their foals and what colors to breed together to produce foals with particular markings. They've learned a lot about how horses pass on their traits to their offspring. But many a foal still manages to surprise a mare's owner when it's born with a completely different color than expected!

Even though horse color is bewildering, there are two things every horse girl knows for sure. She would definitely agree with the old saying "a good horse is never a bad color." The other thing she knows for sure is *exactly* what her favorite horse color is! What's yours? Check out this section and see if your favorite color is here.

Black + Red (and a Dash of White)

Lots of horses are what you'd think of as one-color horses. A horse like this is pretty much covered with one color on most of his body, not including his mane and tail. Many a horse girl has worn out the various shades of brown crayons or colored pencils in her possession (not to mention the black ones!) by drawing these horses.

Scientists who study horse color point out that the whole spectrum is based on the colors red and black, which can be mixed, matched, and watered down, or "diluted," to produce horses of different colors and shades. Toss in some white in the form of patches, spots, and markings, and you've got an amazing variety of patterns and possibilities to choose from!

Chestnut

A chestnut horse is a reddish brown horse that doesn't have black "points." (Points are a horse's legs, mane, and tail.) A chestnut's mane and tail may be the same color as its body or a shade that's darker or lighter, but never black.

As for that coat, it can look red, orange, coppery, or golden. Some chestnuts are very light in color, while others are very dark. A very deep red "liver chestnut" may be so dark it looks black, but if you look closely at its legs you'll see they're dark brown, not black.

Horse people describe chestnuts in many ways. A chestnut horse with a pale mane and tail, for example, is often called a "flaxen." A light chestnut horse is a "sorrel" in the western United States.

Bay

A bay horse has a red-brown or red-yellow coat with black points. Its muzzle and ear tips may also be black. The different shades of bay have special names. A dark red bay, for example, is known as a "blood bay." An orangey bay horse is called a "copper bay."

A bay foal isn't born with black legs. Its legs darken throughout its first year until they finally turn black. Many bay horses also have white markings, such as socks, on their legs.

Black

A black horse is black all over, not counting any white markings on its legs or face. Some black horses are born gray-black and turn pitch-black after shedding their baby hair. Also, some dark brown or bay foals really are black horses in disguise! Black Beauty is an example of a black horse. So is the Black Stallion.

Brown

When is a black horse not a black horse? When it's a brown horse! A "brown horse" in horse-talk is a horse with a blend of brown and black hairs on its body, but lighter, copper hair on its muzzle and parts of its sides and belly. You can often see the areas of copper coloring when sunlight picks them out on the horse's body.

Really dark brown horses are often dubbed "seal brown" in the United States. In Great Britain, they're called "black and tans."

If you ever watch a movie starring a black horse and notice that it sometimes looks brown in places, it may actually be a very dark brown horse.

Gray

Ever hear the saying "The old gray mare, she ain't what she used to be"? When it comes to that mare's color, this saying is definitely true! She may have started out life as a black foal, a chestnut foal, or even a polka-dotted foal!

Gray is made up of a mixture of dark hairs and white hairs scattered across a horse's body. A foal that's going to be gray when it grows up starts "graying" while it's still young. The first signs of gray show up on its face and head. Then the top part of the body starts graying. Many grays keep getting grayer and grayer as the years go by until they're completely white.

One famous gray stage is called "dapple gray." A dapple gray is covered with round, pale rings so that it looks as if it's polka-dotted. Another gray display is called "flea-bitten gray." A flea-bitten gray isn't suffering from bug bites. The "bites" are just flecks of dark color spattered on a pale gray or white coat.

White

White horses are favorites in myths and stories. The mythical flying horse Pegasus was white, and so was Silver, the Lone Ranger's famous horse. Paintings of kings, queens, generals, George Washington, and other famous people in history often show them perched on prancing white horses.

Which is kind of funny, because in real life, a truly white horse is rare. Most white horses are really gray horses who faded to white as they got older. Or they're off-white horses with pink skin and blue eyes called "cremellos." Or they're pintos whose white patches cover most of their bodies. They can even be "few spots"—a term for Appaloosas with so few spots that they're mostly white!

So just what is a truly white horse? A truly white horse is white all over, from the tips of its ears to the tip of its tail. It has pink skin and dark eyes.

Albino Horses?

An albino doesn't have any "pigment," or color, at all.

Sometimes, you'll hear people call a white horse an "albino." But there's actually no such thing as an albino horse! As pink-skinned and white-coated as a white horse may be, it never has pink or red eyes, like albino bunnies or rats.

But that doesn't stop people from calling white horses "albinos"!

Pass the Cremello!

"Cremello" sounds like a kind of dessert or candy. But in horse-talk, it refers to genes that change chestnut, bay, brown, and black into paler colors. Thanks to these genes, horse girls have even *more* horse colors to pick as favorites!

Among these beautiful horses is one that's actually called a cremello. A cremello horse has off-white hair, pink skin, and pale blue eyes. Another popular, pretty color is palomino. A palomino is gold with a white mane and tail.

A third well-known color is buckskin. Most people think of a horse like the star of *Spirit: Stallion of the Cimarron* when they hear "buckskin": a golden horse with black points. But buckskins can also be yellow, off-white, or off-black.

Taffy Time

"Taffy" sounds even more like a sweet than "cremello" does! Again, in horse-talk, it's something else altogether. It's a kind of coloring that mainly affects a horse's black hairs.

Taffies are called "silver dapples" in the United States, but the name is also used for one particular type of taffy. A "silver dapple taffy" is a horse with a chocolatey brown coat spangled with silver dapples and off-white mane and tail. This color blooms on a horse with a mix of black and taffy in its genes.

What if this chocolate-colored horse doesn't have dapples? Then it gets the most candy-like name of any horse: It's called a chocolate taffy! (It may also be called a chocolate flax.)

Brown plus taffy adds up to blue taffy. Picture a chocolatey blue-black horse with a silvery mane and tail, and you'll have an idea of what a blue taffy looks like.

Roan Tones

Like a gray, a roan horse has a coat that's a mixture of dark hairs and white hairs. But unlike a gray, there are usually about as many dark hairs as white hairs. A roan also doesn't get lighter as it gets older, like a gray does. Once a roan—always a roan!

Another difference between grays and roans is that a roan's head and points are the same colors as its dark hairs. A roan's color name is a blend of this "base" color and the word "roan." A chestnut roan, for example, has red chestnut hairs mixed with white hairs. (This color is also called "strawberry roan.") A black roan has black and white hairs. (This color is also called "blue roan.")

Are We Dun Yet?

No, we're not! We can't leave out the duns. Dun horses have pale versions of basic horse colors, like the "cremello" horses. But they've got something special, too: They always have special markings called "primitive markings."

Primitive markings are like the ones prehistoric horses may have sported. (You can see them on the only "true" wild horse left in the world—the Przewalski's horse of Mongolia.) One of these markings is a dorsal stripe running down a dun's back from withers to tail. Another is a splash of darker coloring on the horse's nose or face that is called a mask. A dun often has some stripes on its legs, too.

You can take your pick of four main colors when it comes to duns. Red duns, as you might guess, are reddish. Mouse duns are muddy brown. Yellow duns are pale yellow or tan. Blue duns range from blue gray to silver. This color is also called "grullo" or "grulla."

The Spotted Wonder

Many gray Thoroughbred racehorses descend from a horse called The Tetrarch. The Tetrarch was a big, strong gray colt splotched with blobs of white. Before his first race as a two-year-old in 1913, people at the racetrack laughed at him and said he looked like a spotted rocking horse.

But the laughing stopped when the colt blazed to victory in every race he ran that year. His amazing speed wowed people and even scared off competitors. An injury to a leg ended his racing career early, so he didn't run at age three—but he enjoyed a long, lazy life at a farm and fathered many great racehorses.

Painted Ponies!

> ## Paint or Pinto?
>
> A paint is always a pinto—but a pinto isn't always a paint! A paint horse is a breed. Its ancestors include Quarter Horses, Thoroughbreds, or both. "Pinto" is a color pattern. A horse who's a pinto can be any breed.

Spot, Patches, Ol' Paint—they're all good names for the splashy horses called "pintos."

A pinto is a horse with a pattern of white and patches of any other color on its body. If you shaved off a pinto's hair, you'd find pink skin under the white patches and colored skin under the colored patches. (You'd also have a chilly, irritated horse.)

Horse people divvy up pintos by their patterns. As you might guess, they have different names for all these pattern groups! See if you can "spot" your favorite pinto in this parade of painted ponies.

Tobiano

A tobiano horse looks as if a bucket of white paint were poured onto his back from above. His white markings drip down from his crest, withers, and backbone. He may have just a few dribbles of white running down from this "top line" of his body, or he may have large areas of white. A tobiano may also be totally white except for his head!

A "toby" also has four white legs. His hooves can be pale or dark. The top of his tail is often white. His face may have white markings that are like the stars and blazes you might see on a solid-colored horse. Tobiano is the most common kind of pinto coloring.

Frame Overo

"Overo" is a word used for a bunch of pintos who aren't tobianos. One of the best known kinds is the frame overo. A frame overo's white markings don't drip down from her spine or splash up from her belly. Instead, she looks a little like she went through a car wash, where the brushes dabbed white paint on her! The white, jagged patches mainly run across the horse's neck and sides.

Why the "frame" in the name? Because a frame overo has a border of color around most of her body, with white across her sides and neck. The colored parts look a bit like a picture frame around the white patches.

Sabino

A sabino horse is like an upside-down tobiano. The white runs up his body instead of down, making him look as if he stepped into a tub of white paint.

A sabino can also be mostly a color with a few splotches of white. The white patches often have lacy edges. Some sabinos have just a few patches of white on the belly or under the neck.

Most sabinos have white legs and hooves, and the white markings often stretch high up the legs. A river of white runs down the face, and a white spot on the chin makes it look as if the horse dipped it in milk.

Splashed White

Okay, all pintos look as if they've been splashed with white—so why is there a pinto that's called splashed white?

If a sabino looks as if it *waded* in white paint, a splashed white, which is rare, often looks as if it went *swimming* in the stuff—and put its head "underwater," too!

A splashed white's dark patches have very smooth edges, as if they were drawn with brand-new felt-tip pens. (A sabino's dark patches may look lacy, as if drawn with a crayon.) The tail tip is often white. The legs often are, too. A "splash" may also have a white face and blue eyes.

Piebalds

Black-and-white patched horses are often called "piebalds." Horses patched with white and any other color are known as "skewbalds." Officially, these terms are considered old-fashioned, but many people still use them.

Spotted Horses

"Whoa," you might say at this point. "Wait a minute. *Spotted horses?* Weren't we just talking about spotted horses?"

Well, yes and no. Technically, a pinto isn't "spotted"—it's "pied" or "broken colored." (Or as they say in England, "odd-colored.") A *spotted* horse actually has a spattering of dots on its coat. It may have a dark coat spangled with white polka dots, or a pale coat dotted with dark ones.

SPOT THE DIFFERENCE

Spotted horses sometimes change their patterns as they get older.

"Appaloosa complex"

There's a wide range of spot patterns. A horse may be polka-dotted all over, like a Dalmatian. Another spotted horse may have small spots so close together that it looks as if snow fell on its back. Yet another horse may have several patterns going on.

Horse people lump all these patterns in one group called "Appaloosa complex" or "leopard complex." (But English horse people call it "tiger spotting"! Hmm. Anybody up for "cheetah chips" or "ocelot dots"?)

No matter how their spots are sprinkled, spotted horses have a few things in common. They have spotted skin, and their face and parts of their bellies are mottled. They have striped hooves, except on legs with white leg markings. And you can see the whites of their eyes all the time—not just when they're scared or angry!

Seeing Spots?

A horse can have both broken coloring *and* spots! A horse like this is called a "pintaloosa." Talk about seeing spots before your eyes!

Spot On!

Horse people use different words to describe the patterns of spotted horses. Some of the names are leopard, snowflake, varnish, blanket, and few-spot.

They're useful names because each one gives you a good idea of what the horse looks like. "Leopard," for example, describes a white horse spattered with dark spots. "Snowflake" is a white-spotted pattern. A "spotted blanket" is a polka-dotted white patch on a horse's rump.

Some breeds of horses are famous for their spots. The most famous is the Appaloosa. Appaloosas were beloved by the Nez Perce Indians of the northwestern United States, who bred them and prized them for their colors. The breed's name is linked to that of a river, the Palouse, which runs through the Nez Perces' homeland. The Pony of the Americas is also a spotted breed. It got its start with a stallion who was half Appaloosa and half Shetland pony.

Another famous spotted breed is the Knabstrupper. This breed comes from Denmark. It's a white horse with black or brown egg-shaped spots all over its body. It's pretty popular as a circus horse!

Knabstrupper

What's in a Name?

The Nez Perce Indians didn't call their horses "Appaloosas." Their word for horse was "sik'em," and they called the spotted breed "m'a min." Then again, the Nez Perce didn't call themselves "Nez Perce," either. This name was given to them by explorers.

Sophie Says: My favorite horse color is a red chestnut with slightly gold tints to the mane and tail, three white socks or stockings of different lengths, and a large white blaze running down the center of the face, ending on the muzzle.

Stars and Stripes!

Now let's take a look at just the colors and patterns on a horse's face and legs.

These parts of a horse's body have their own set of markings. The markings are white, and the skin under them is pink. (White hair in these markings, like the patches on pintos, grows out of pink skin. Grays and roans are the only horses with white hair growing out of dark skin.)

Every horse's white markings are different. They're often used to identify individual horses in a wild-horse herd or on registration papers. Some horses have lots of white markings, while others have just a tiny bit of white or none at all.

As you might guess, horse people have a lot of names for these markings! Here's a list of the white markings you might see next time you visit a stable.

Face Markings

Bald face or white face: a white blaze that spills over the sides of the horse's face and often over one or both eyes (depending on its shape, this blaze may also be called an apron face or bonnet face)

Blaze: a wide white marking that runs down a horse's face to its nostrils

Connected or joined markings: white markings connected by thin ribbons of white

Race: a crooked strip

Snip: a dab of white between a horse's nostrils

Star: a patch of white on a horse's forehead, between its eyes

Strip or stripe: a skinny streak of white down a horse's face

White muzzle: no surprise here—it's a white muzzle (sometimes called a milk-bucket muzzle)

Star   *Strip or Stripe*   *Blaze*   *Bald face or white face*

Leg Markings

Coronet: the thin white band or line right where the hoof meets the leg

Ermine spots: black or brown spots on a leg with white markings near the hoof

Half-stocking: white that reaches halfway up the lower leg; a three-quarter stocking almost reaches the hock or knee

Heel: a dollop of white on the heel; less than that and it's a half-heel

Pastern: white that covers the pastern, the part between the hoof and the fetlock; if it only covers half this area, it's a half-pastern, and if it goes up past the pastern, it's a high pastern (also called a fetlock or ankle; lots of names for one little mark!)

Sock: white that reaches above the fetlock but below the lower leg's halfway point

Stocking: white that reaches the knee or hock

White crown: white on the front of the pastern

White leg: white that reaches the top of the leg

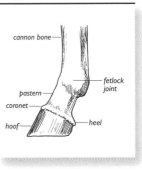

cannon bone

fetlock joint

pastern

coronet

hoof

heel

Pastern   Half-stocking   Stocking   Ermine spots

Hoof Prints

A horse's hoof color is linked to the skin color of the leg above it—specifically, from the thin band called the coronet or coronary band.

A hoof attached to a pink-skinned, white leg is pale in color. A leg that's black or any other color has a dark gray or black hoof. Some horses, however, have striped hooves. Appaloosas and other spotted horses always do. A horse with ermine spots on the coronet of a white leg may have striped hooves, too.

Many horse people have strong opinions about the colors of horses' hooves. It's widely believed, for example, that dark hooves are stronger than pale hooves. Studies show no difference.

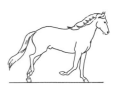

Top Ten Funny Horse Color Terms!

Some horse color terms are just plain weird.

Bloody buttocks: *Not* a terrible injury to a horse's backside! "Blood markings" are areas of "fleabites" on a flea-bitten gray that are so close together they form patches of color.

Chicken feet: A web of dark stripes on a horse's forehead.

Eel stripe: Another name for a dorsal stripe, which runs along some horses' spines.

Ghost markings: Spooky? Nah. Just pale primitive markings on a foal that fade away as it grows.

Medicine hat: *Not* a healing cap you put on a horse. It's a pinto who's mostly white with a splash of color on top of its head.

Nose rug: This won't keep your horse's snout warm. It refers to a "mask" of dark hair on a horse's face.

Pinkie syndrome: Horses don't have pinkies. The "pinkie" in this syndrome refers to gray horses who lose color in their skin as they get older. They often develop pale pink muzzles and eye rims.

Ticking: A horse with lots of ticking isn't covered with bugs—it's just spattered with specks of white hair! Ticking looks like what you'd get if you flicked white paint off a paintbrush onto a horse's coat.

Toad face: Sounds like you're insulting your horse, but it refers to a sand-colored or "mealy" muzzle.

Zebra stripes: Zebras have them—and some horses have them on their legs, too.

Horse Hide

A horse's color is, in a way, just "decoration." The horse's skin and hair, however, have real jobs. They keep the horse warm in cold weather and cool in hot weather.

A typical horse's skin is nearly an inch (2.5 cm) thick on much of its body. But if you've ever groomed a horse, you know it has lots of ticklish or sensitive spots—usually on its head and belly. In these places, the skin is much thinner.

A horse has two kinds of hair. One kind forms an outer coat that helps shed rain. The other forms an inner coat that helps keep the horse warm.

A horse's summer coat is sleeker than his winter coat. The winter coat has longer hairs and is fluffy. Many horses' winter coats are a different color than their summer coats. They're often darker (though some horses buck this trend and turn lighter!). Roans are especially well known for changing colors throughout the year.

Horse hair is usually short and straight, but some horses have curly hair.

The Bashkir Curly (also called the American Curly) is famous for its soft, fine coat of ringlets. Its silky mane and tail is curly, too.

Flat-coated horses often have curls and swirls in their hair, as well. They are like the cowlicks in people's hair and are called "whorls."

Horse Feathers

Pegasus isn't the only horse with feathers! "Feathers" is what horse people call long hair that drapes over some horses' hooves. Shires and Clydesdales are two breeds famous for their feathers.

Hairy Horse

A horse has from 800 to 1,200 outer-coat hairs and from 1,200 to 2,000 inner-coat hairs in just one square inch (2.5 cm) of skin.

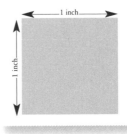

Fiery Redheads?

Around the world and throughout history, people have come up with notions about horses, colors, and markings. They've linked them to superstitious beliefs about good luck and bad luck, for example. They've also linked them to horses' personalities and temperaments.

"Temperament" refers to a horse's way of behaving and reacting to its world. If your horse is excitable and anxious, you might say she has a nervous temperament. If she's bombproof, you might say she's calm.

Some people are convinced that chestnut horses are fiery, super-sensitive, and "hot-blooded"—like the mare Ginger in *Black Beauty*.

Other horse-color stereotypes include the notion that piebalds are calm and cooperative, duns are tough, roans are lazy, and black horses are wild and dangerous (think Black Stallion!). But for every person who thinks one way about a color, you'll likely meet another who thinks the opposite. Scientists are finding out cool things about animals, their colors, and behavior—so maybe in the future there'll be some facts to think about alongside these far-fetched fancies!

Quick! Tie This Knot!

Here's a great skill to learn now if you're going to spend time around horses—how to tie a quick-release knot.

Sure, in movies you always see people just looping their horses' reins around trees or a hitching post. But in real life, that's not a great idea. If the horse pulls hard to get away, he'll break the reins. Now you've got broken reins *and* a loose horse!

A horse is tied with a quick-release knot for two good reasons. For one thing, the knot won't get tighter if he pulls on the rope. (Ever try to untie a tightly stuck knot? You don't want to be picking at a stubborn knot with a frightened or impatient horse at the other end of it!)

Secondly, you can untie a quick-release knot with just one tug. This is very important, especially if the horse is freaking out or if there's an emergency that requires you to free your horse fast.

You might use this knot when you tie up the horse to saddle and bridle it, groom it, or before and after a ride. But you don't want to try tying this knot for the first time when it's attached to a horse. So get a length of rope (or twine, or a dog leash, or even your bathrobe belt) and practice first. (A short rope won't work—get one at least three feet/one meter long.) Then find a post—such as a fence post or rail, a table leg, a tree—or a C-shaped cabinet or drawer handle.

Can't find a long-enough rope? Don't despair. Grab a string or a shoelace! Tie one end around a model horse's neck, and loop the other end through the handle of a coffee mug to practice the knot.

(Note: There are different kinds of quick-release knots—this one is a simple version. Practice tying it so that eventually you never have to put your fingers into any of the loops you make: In real life, you could get hurt this way if a horse pulled back on the rope. And yes, you can switch the directions around if you're a lefty.)

P.S. The Web and books are full of diagrams in which spaghetti-like strands of rope intertwine and magically become A Knot; one of the most straightforward and practical demonstrations I've found online is a video showing a knot approved by the British Horse Society. You'll find it on YouTube at this website: www.youtube.com/watch?v=3XFO d SsvE. (Better yet, get a real, live horse handler to show you how.)

Step 1. Hold the rope in both hands. Pretend the horse is attached to the end of the rope that's in your left hand. We'll call this the "horse rope." The end of the rope that's in your right hand is the "free end."

Step 2. Use your right hand to pull the rope by its free end around the post or through the handle.

Step 3. Fold the free end in half so that you make a small loop. Hold the loop closed with your right hand.

Step 4. Lay the loop on top of the horse rope. Hold the loop against the horse rope by pinching them in place with your thumb and index finger.

Step 5. Use your left hand to push the loop over the horse rope, around it, and then up again. It will pop up inside the circle formed by the whole rope being looped around the post.

Step 6. Hold the horse rope firmly with your left hand while tugging the loop up with your right hand. This will make the circle get smaller as the knot slides toward the post. But don't drag the free end of the rope through the circle, or it'll all fall apart!

Step 7. Now pretend you're a restless horse and pull on the horse rope. Does the knot stay tied?

Step 8. Release your horse! Pull on the free end of the rope. The knot should slide open easily.

Caution: Some horses and ponies are quick-escape artists who can figure out how to undo a quick-release knot. There are ways to outfox these sneaky steeds. If you take riding lessons, ask your instructor to show you how.

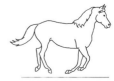

HORSE-TORY: AN EQUINE TIMELINE

THE VERY FIRST HORSES

Horses weren't always the long-tailed, swept-mane, velvety-muzzled creatures they are today. You wouldn't have even recognized their little runty ancestors if you traveled back in time about 55 million years ago— a mere 10 million years after the last dinosaurs became extinct.

Back then, the horse's ancestor was an animal about the size of a small dog. It walked on four-toed front feet and three-toed hind feet. It ate leaves and lived in forests in North America and parts of Europe.

In 1876, the scientists who dug up this small animal's fossils in North America named it "Eohippus"—a pretty word that means "dawn horse."

But its name was later changed to *Hyracotherium*. Why? Because it turned out another scientist had already discovered dawn-horse fossils in Europe in 1841, and he'd already given them the name *Hyracotherium*.

In science, a fossil is stuck with the first name it gets. So *Hyracotherium* is the horse's official name. It means "hyrax-like beast." (Okay, so . . . what's a hyrax? It's a rabbit-size African animal that's related to the elephant!)

What's *That?*

Imagine that you've never seen a horse before. What would you call this big, lively animal if it suddenly showed up on your doorstep?

That's what happened to native people in parts of the world long ago, when European explorers landed on their shores and unloaded horses. They had to come up with names for these new creatures.

In Hawaii, horses first came ashore from ships in 1803 or 1804. The islanders called them "wa'a a holo honua," which means "canoes that travel on land"! Hawaiians used canoes, so it made sense to describe horses in this way. Later, the islanders called the horse "lio nui," which pretty much means "big four-legged animal."

When Europeans arrived in Australia, they were astonished to see kangaroos and koala bears. But the native Australians, known as Aborigines, were just as surprised to see horses when the first ones arrived in 1788. In some parts of Australia, Aborigines called the horse "yarraman," which may come from a word they used for "teeth." (Invented by a person who was bitten by a horse, maybe?) In other places, they called horses "pindi nanto," which means "the newcomer's kangaroo"!

Horses Evolve

About 35 million years ago, the horse's ancestors were a little bigger than *Hyracotherium*. They walked on just three of their four front toes. Scientists dubbed this animal *Mesohippus*, which means "middle horse." This name is right on target because *Mesohippus* was a little like horses that lived before it, but also a bit like modern horses.

Another important horse ancestor is pony-sized *Parahippus*, which lived more than 20 million years ago. *Parahippus* means "side horse," but it's unclear exactly what the "side" refers to—maybe its teeth or its side toes.

What scientists *do* know is that this horse's face and teeth were more like a modern horse's. It could eat grass as well as leaves—which was a good thing, because North America was changing, too. Grasslands were spreading across land that was once covered by forests and swamps.

Parahippus ran across these lands on three-toed feet, but carried most of its weight on just one toe of each foot. The single hooves of horses were starting to develop!

Eohippus / Hyracotherium	Mesohippus	Parahippus	Merychippus
55–45 million years ago	*37–32 million years ago*	*24–17 million years ago*	*17–11 million years ago*

Getting Closer . . .

About 17 million years ago, an even more horsey-looking horse scampered across North America. Scientists call it *Merychippus*. This name has nothing to do with feeling merry. It means "ruminant horse."

A ruminant is an animal, like a cow, that swallows grass, then coughs it back up to chew it some more before swallowing it again. No horse in history has ever done this, but *Merychippus* wasn't asked for its opinion when it was mistakenly so named.

Like *Parahippus*, *Merychippus* had long legs for speed, a long neck that helped it graze on grass, and a long face that let it watch for danger while grazing.

Horses Galore!

One of *Merychippus*'s descendants was *Dinohippus*. This name means "powerful horse." Scientists have found clues in its skeleton that show its muscles and leg bones could "lock in place" so that it could stand around without using any energy—and even sleep standing up—much like modern horses.

Dinohippus lived in North America until about five million years ago.

But *Dinohippus* wasn't the only "grandchild" of *Merychippus*. A few other species were trotting around, too. One of them was a big horse that lived about two million years ago in South America. This horse, called *Hippidion,* was about the size of a huge plow horse or workhorse. Oddly, its name means "pony"! Even odder, it may have had a rubbery, snout-like muzzle, sort of like a pig or tapir. It died out about 10,000 years ago.

Modern horses are known as *Equus,* which simply means "horse." *Equus* have been around for about five million years. The group *Equus* includes not only horses but also zebras and asses. (Yes, it's okay to say that word when referring to horse relatives!) Wild asses live in parts of Africa and Asia. The domestic ones are called donkeys.

Horses Come and Horses Go

If you traveled a few million years back in time, you'd be able to *walk* from Alaska to Russia. Back then, a bridge of land connected these two places. Early horses used it to travel back and forth between North America, Europe, and Asia.

This handy route was wiped out when the Ice Age had a meltdown about 11,000 years ago. Huge areas of the ice sheets that spread across the land melted. The water ran into the oceans and made them deeper. The land bridge vanished underwater.

The horses in Europe and Asia (as well as the zebra's ancestors in Africa) survived, but something weird happened to horses in North America. They disappeared! Over time, they simply died out. Scientists aren't yet sure just why this happened. North America was sadly lacking in horses until the early 1500s, when Spanish explorers brought them over from Europe in ships.

ON THE ROAD TO HORSES

Old diagrams of horse history show the different kinds of horses marching through time, with small, ancient horses growing steadily larger until they look like modern horses. They also switch from eating leaves to eating grass, and lose their toes in an orderly manner as they evolve one-toed hooves.

But scientists have since learned that this line-up is too simple. Horses didn't change in such a direct way. Fossil teeth and jaws, for example, show that many ancient horses may have readily eaten both grass and leaves, depending on what they could find.

Horses didn't grow steadily larger over time, either. Horses that lived from 5 million to 24 million years ago varied in size. Some were as small as little dogs while others were big enough to saddle up!

Toes did not disappear at a steady pace, either. Some kinds of horses still had three toes when other kinds of horses had already lost their extras.

Horse, Meet Human!

Prehistoric people saw horses as "fast food"! They hunted them as they hunted other animals. Nobody knows how humans figured out that horses could be tamed and used to pull carts, plow fields, or carry loads—and riders!

But we have a pretty good idea of when horses and humans teamed up. This knowledge is based on the work of archaeologists—people who study how humans lived in the past. They've dug up—literally!—lots of clues. These clues show that horses were kept by people about 5,700 years ago. They found the clues in parts of Eurasia, a vast area of land where Europe and Asia meet.

One important clue was the discovery of ancient fenced-in areas, or "corrals," in Kazakhstan, a country that lies south of Russia. The corrals are

I DIG HORSES!

You can dig up pictures of horse fossils and find more on how scientists learned about horse history from this website: www.flmnh.ufl.edu/fhc/Stratmap1.htm.

about 5,600 years old. Scientists found that the soil in the corrals contained minerals you'd expect to find in a place once filled with horse manure.

Scientists also studied ancient pots found in the area. They discovered that the pots once held mare's milk. Nobody would ever try to milk a wild mare, so the milk must have come from domestic ones. (Mare's milk is still popular in Kazakhstan today.)

Girls on Horseback

After people started riding horses, girls must have figured out rather quickly that life on horseback would be pretty cool, too! But as you probably know, girls in many parts of the world haven't always had the choices and chances they enjoy in many places today.

Girls and women started out riding astride like boys and men—with one leg on either side of the horse. But in western Europe, about 1,500 years ago, upper-class people (the ones who were wealthy enough to own horses) decided that riding astride wasn't "ladylike" for girls and ladies wearing dresses. If your family was rich enough to own a horse and saddle, you rode *sidesaddle*.

Sitting Sideways

In the days of knights on horse-back, ladies' sidesaddles were like big, stuffed pillows on a wooden base. If you sat in this saddle, you faced sideways and put your feet on a little platform. Most likely, some-body else held your horse's reins and led you. (And that's if you were allowed to ride yourself! Often, a woman "rode pillion," which means she sat on a pad behind the saddle—which was occupied by a man.)

By the late 1300s, ladies began facing forward while riding— putting just the left foot on the platform instead of both feet. By now, though, some European women daringly rode astride horses by wearing long skirts that were split to make this possible (kind of like an early version of "skorts").

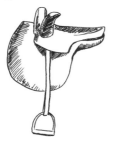

A Queen's Bright Idea

The sidesaddle didn't change much until the mid-1500s, when a French queen named Catherine de Medici came up with a great idea. She had an extra bump added to the front of her saddle. Then she put her right knee in between this bump and the one already on the saddle—the part called the "pommel."

By hooking her leg over the saddle in this way, a rider could face forward more easily—and she had better control of her horse.

Astride, Not Aside

In Colonial America, back in the 1600s and 1700s, ladies rode sidesaddle. Girls on the East Coast continued to ride this way up until the very early 1900s.

It's hard to believe, but it was still uncommon for girls and women to ride astride at that time—and some people got really fired up about it. The King of England, for example. In July 1913, he banned women from riding astride in a parade at a big horse show in London.

English newspapers called riding astride an "American cowgirl innovation, which can never appeal to English ladies."

Meanwhile, out west, riding astride wasn't a shocking sight. Pioneer girls often rode astride—and bareback. In towns, however, ladies who wanted to appear refined would ride sidesaddle.

Today, most girls ride astride, but the sidesaddle is still alive and well. Girls and women who ride sidesaddle today do so because they *want* to— not because they *have* to! *Yee-haw!*

Horse Girls in Other Countries

While girls in western Europe and North America were riding sidesaddle, girls in other places were already riding astride (which is sometimes called "cross-saddle"). Artwork created in Asia nearly 2,000 years ago shows women riding astride their horses. Girls rode just like boys as they thundered across the grasslands of central Asia on their ponies. In India, females also rode astride. Women in Mexico and South America rode astride, too.

When horses arrived in North America in the 1500s, the Plains Indians quickly learned to ride them—and the women rode like the men.

✦ TOP TEN HISTORIC HORSES!

Bucephalus (from about 355 BC to 326 BC), the black warhorse of Alexander the Great, a king who ruled ancient Greece about 2,300 years ago. Alexander was only about ten years old when he tamed the big, fierce horse, allegedly by turning him away from the sun so he wouldn't be scared by his shadow.

Babieca (?–1101), the white Andalusian stallion ridden by a Spanish warrior named El Cid, who rode him for about thirty years in battle. Babieca lived for two years after El Cid died and was allegedly buried alongside him.

Brown Beauty, a name often used to describe the mare that Paul Revere borrowed to ride from Charlestown to Lexington in Massachusetts on April 18, 1775, at the start of the American Revolutionary War, to announce, "The British are coming!"

Marengo (1793–1831), a gray Arabian who carried Napoleon I, emperor of France, safely through many battles. He was the most famous of Napoleon's warhorses.

Bloated Jaw (mid-1800s), the chestnut warhorse of Chief Sitting Bull, leader of the Dakota Sioux in the western United States. His other horse was a black stallion named Blackie.

Traveller (1857–1872), the gray warhorse ridden by General Robert E. Lee of the Confederate Army during the American Civil War. Lee praised his steady, sure-footed horse as a wise, brave, and affectionate comrade.

Cincinnati (1860–1878), the dark bay horse ridden by General Ulysses S. Grant of the Union Army during the American Civil War. Grant loved horses and was an excellent rider. He let just a few other people ride Cincinnati—and one of those riders was Abraham Lincoln.

Comanche (1862?–1891), a bay or buckskin gelding remembered as the only U.S. Army survivor of the Battle of the Little Big Horn, fought between the army and Native Americans in Montana on June 25, 1876.

Grey Dawn (early 1900s), a white horse ridden on March 3, 1913, by lawyer Inez Mulholland, in a parade in Washington, D.C., that was dedicated to demanding that women be given the right to vote. Women finally got the right to vote in 1920.

Black Jack (1947–1976), a black gelding who was the last horse to wear the brand of the U.S. Army. He worked as a caparisoned (riderless) horse in official parades, carrying an empty saddle with a pair of boots stuck backward into the stirrups to honor heroes who had died.

The Pony Express

In 1859, it could take more than a month for a letter to travel from the eastern United States to California. That's because it had to travel much of the way in a wagon.

But from 1860 to 1861, some U.S. mail made the trip in just eight days thanks to the Pony Express.

The Pony Express carried mail from St. Louis, Missouri, to California. Horses and riders galloped at top speed. The rider stopped at stations along the way to change horses. At some stations, the rider stopped, too, and passed the mailbags to the next rider. The Pony Express ended when telegraph lines were strung coast-to-coast, and news that needed to travel quickly could be transmitted using electrical signals instead of on paper.

Ode to Horses

Look back at our struggle for freedom,
Trace our present day's strength to its source;
And you'll find that man's pathway to glory
Is strewn with the bones of a horse.

—*by an anonymous horse lover*

Running Free

Horses in the Wild

Horses descend from wild ancestors. Horses still *act* like their wild ancestors, and some breeds even look a lot like them.

But do any horses still *live* like their wild ancestors (not counting horse cousins like zebras and wild asses)?

You'll be glad to hear that yes, they do—though funnily enough, they have humans to thank for their wildness.

Feral Horses

What is a feral horse? "Feral" comes from an old Latin word that also means "wild animal." Today, this word is used mainly to describe a domestic animal that has escaped and gone wild.

To understand what's wild and what's feral, it's important to know just what "domestic" means. "Domestic" describes a kind of animal that has been specially bred, for many generations, to be kept, used, and raised by people. Out of all the world's animals, only about two dozen are domestic. Dogs, cats, and horses are among them.

A domestic animal is tame, but not all tame animals are domesticated! A wild animal, like a wolf or zebra, can be tamed and kept in a zoo, or a baby wild animal can be raised by people and kept tame. But its ancestors weren't specially bred to produce tame animals that can live with people. The animal may be tame, but it's still wild—even if it doesn't act wild.

That's where "feral" comes into play—and why "wild" horses are technically feral horses. Horses have been domesticated for thousands of years. Horses that live in the wild today are descended from domestic animals that escaped or were let loose in the past.

That said, we're going to go ahead and call them "wild horses" anyway—it honors the wild spirit that still lies deep inside them.

Where Wild Horses Roam

Wild horses can still be found in parts of Canada and in Central and South America. A popular South American horse breed, the Criollo, descends from these wild horses. Wild horses also roam Puerto Rico's Vieques Island.

Wild Horses in North America

Mustangs are *the* horses people think of when they picture wild horses. Carmakers admired the mustang so much, they even named a slick car after it!

Mustangs descend from domestic horses who escaped or were set free over the past four hundred years. Some of these ancestors were Spanish horses brought to America by explorers more than four hundred years ago. A few bands of nearly pure Spanish horses are scattered across the West today in protected areas set aside for them.

Altogether, there are about 29,000 mustangs roaming the western United States at this time; about half of them live in Nevada. Some of them live on land that is privately owned by people who want to provide land for mustangs to roam. But most mustangs live on lands that are managed by a government agency called the Bureau of Land Management, or BLM.

The BLM is in charge of U.S. public lands—all the land that belongs to the U.S. government. This land includes grasslands, forests, and deserts, and many wild lands. Part of the BLM's job is divvying up how the land is used by people and animals—including mustangs.

Since 1971, the BLM has also been in charge of managing wild horses and burros in the West. This job involves keeping the number of horses in balance with the land so that the horses get enough to eat without harming the land or the other animals that eat plants, too. The "other animals" include wild animals, such as deer, but also domestic ones, such as cattle.

Managing the horses' numbers involves rounding up herds and selling some of the horses because there may be too many of them in one place. Today, the BLM is keeping some 33,000 captured wild horses in pens, having removed them from lands where they once roamed free. Horses have also been killed to control their numbers. The BLM's management of wild horses is a controversial issue—there are people who support the BLM's plans, and others who feel strongly that the agency is not doing a good job of protecting the animals.

Visiting Wild Horses

Want to visit wild horses on refuges and public lands across North America? Check out *The American Mustang Guidebook* by Lisa Dines. It tells you where to find them and also how to adopt and gentle a mustang.

Adopt a Mustang!

The BLM (Bureau of Land Management) has about as many mustangs in captivity as there are in the wild. These horses were rounded up because the BLM controls how many mustangs can live in certain areas. Many of these mustangs are too old or wild to be tamed. They are kept in "long-term" holding facilities.

Other captive mustangs are kept in "short-term" facilities. These horses are tamed and then put up for adoption through the BLM's "Adopt a Wild Horse or Burro" program. More than 235,000 wild horses and burros have been adopted since this program got started in the 1970s!

Mustangs have found new lives as police horses, cowhorses, and riding horses. They're used by some Border Patrol officials as well as the U.S. Marine Corps.

Unfortunately, right now there are lots of mustangs ready for adoption but not enough people ready to adopt them. If you'd like to find out more about adopting wild horses, visit the BLM's Wild Horse and Burro Adoption website: **www.blm.gov/wo/st/en/prog/wild_horse_and_burro/What_We_Do/wild_horse_and_burro0.html**.

Wild Horse Annie

In the late 1800s and early 1900s, about two million mustangs lived in the grasslands of the United States. Many cattle ranchers didn't want them competing with their cattle for food and water, and many farmers also thought they were pests. As a result, mustangs were rounded up in ways that were very cruel and treated badly afterward.

The mistreatment of mustangs horrified a woman named Velma Johnston when she saw it firsthand in the 1950s. She fought to get laws passed to protect mustangs. She urged kids to write letters to members of Congress. The plan worked—Congress was flooded with letters! In 1959, the "Save the Mustangs" bill was passed.

This law made it illegal to chase and shoot mustangs from airplanes, cars, and other motorized vehicles. It also made it illegal to poison watering holes that mustangs used. Johnston, now known as "Wild Horse Annie," was pleased, but she knew more work needed to be done.

Eleven years later, in 1971, another law was passed. Called the "Wild Free-Roaming Horse and Burro Act," it recognized that mustangs "are living symbols of the pioneer spirit of the West" and that "they enrich the lives of the American people."

Because of this law, mustang herds are now managed by the BLM. People can't just go out on the range, round them up, and take them away. Mustang management today isn't perfect, to be sure—but thanks to Wild Horse Annie, it's definitely a lot better than it used to be. (You can read her life story in the book *Mustang: Wild Spirit of the West* by Marguerite Henry.)

Sea Horses!

Not all wild horses romp across the range. Some of them are beach bums!
Up and down the eastern seaboard of the United States and Canada are
islands where wild ponies roam.

The most famous
of these equine
islanders are the
Chincoteague ponies.
Chincoteague is a
small island off the
coast of Virginia.
The ponies actually
live on the longer,
thinner island of
Assateague, which
stands between
Chincoteague and
the Atlantic Ocean.

According to legend, the ponies descend from Spanish horses that
swam ashore in the 1500s after a shipwreck. But it's more likely that their
ancestors were horses let loose on the island by settlers in the 1600s.

The ponies feed on salty marsh grasses and wander freely through the
woods and along beaches. (They also stroll through campgrounds and try
to snitch treats—we
know one family who
had to shoo away a
pony trying to filch
the bacon they were
cooking!)

Though the ponies
live a wild life, they're
actually owned by the
Chincoteague

READ ALL ABOUT IT!

Read a great horse story and learn about Chincoteague
ponies all at the same time in *Misty of Chincoteague* by
Marguerite Henry. She also wrote two other island-
pony books: *Stormy, Misty's Foal* and *Sea Star, Orphan
of Chincoteague.*

Volunteer Fire Department, which rounds them up every July. "Saltwater
cowboys" drive the herd into the narrow channel
between the two islands. The ponies swim across and
climb out on shore. They're checked over and a few
foals are sold; then the herd swims back to freedom
the next day.

Wild Horses in Europe

Most people think of the American West when they think of wild horses, but you can also find horses living wild in parts of Europe.

These horses are actually owned by people, but they're allowed to live like wild animals most of the time. Parts of Spain and Portugal, for example, are home to small bands of such half-wild ponies. They live mainly in mountainous areas. In southern France, white Camargue horses run free in a marshy area.

Parts of Great Britain are also famous for their owned-but-wild ponies. The pony breeds often have the same name as their range. This nation's wild ponies include the following breeds: Exmoor ponies, Dartmoor ponies, New Forest ponies, and Lundy ponies.

Wild Horses in Asia and Africa

Asia and Africa are the two largest of the world's seven continents—and both have bragging rights when it comes to wild horses.

Many African grasslands boast large herds of zebras, the striped wild cousins of horses. But Africa's feral horses, about 150 of them, live in the dry, desolate Namib Desert.

Asia's most horse-crazy place is Mongolia, a country about the size of Alaska that's sandwiched between Russia and China. It's home to nearly three million domestic horses—about one for every Mongolian citizen. It also boasts about 325 wild horses—the world-famous Przewalski's horses.

Przewalski's horses are very ancient and have lived in Mongolia for thousands of years. They're said to be the only "truly wild" horses in the world because they've never been domesticated.

Hunting by people caused Przewalski's horses to become extinct by the 1960s. Luckily, some of the horses still lived in zoos, which bred them to boost their numbers. By 1992, there were enough horses to risk setting free a small herd. Since then, more horses have been released, and they're doing well in their "new-old" home.

"PRZEWALSKI"?

"Przewalski"? Now *that's* a mouthful! You pronounce it "sha-val-ski." The Mongolian language has an easier-to-say name for it: *Takhi*, which sounds a little like "tock."

Where the Wild Things Are

Wild about wild horses? There are lots of resources available if you want to find out more about them! Here are a few.

Books:

Among Wild Horses by Lynne Pomeranz

Wild Horses: Galloping Through Time by Kelly Milner Halls

Wild Horses I Have Known by Hope Ryden

Wild Horses: The World's Last Surviving Herds by Elwyn Hartley Edwards

Videos:

Cloud: Wild Stallion of the Rockies

Cloud's Legacy: The Wild Stallion Returns

Cloud: Challenge of the Stallions

Websites:

American Mustang and Burro Association www.ambainc.net

Black Hills Wild Horse Sanctuary www.gwtc.net/~iram

Equus Survival Trust www.equus-survival-trust.org

Return to Freedom American Wild Horse Sanctuary www.returntofreedom.org/sanctuary/spirit.html

Wild Horses: An American Romance www.netnebraska.org/extras/wildhorses

Wild Horses in Australia

"Brumbies" are Australian wild horses. Like mustangs, they descend from horses that escaped from ranches or were let loose by their owners. Brumbies first arrived in Australia in 1788. They were used for farming and ranching.

Today, Australia has more wild horses than any other country—about 300,000 of them.

Many Australians take pride in the brumbies as symbols of Australia's history. But brumbies are also seen as pests that harm the land and its plants and make it hard for wild animals to survive.

Brumbies aren't protected by law as American mustangs are. People are working to stop brumbies from being killed and to come up with better ways to control their numbers. Today, Australia has brumby sanctuaries, and some brumbies are being tamed so they can be adopted.

Clothes-Horses

What Horses Wear

Those lucky wild horses. They don't have to wear a stitch, and they certainly don't wear horseshoes! Domestic horses and their people, however, have all sorts of clothing and gear.

A riding horse's gear is called "tack" or "saddlery." A horse that is driven wears a "harness." Horses have so much gear that a stable needs to store it in a tack room or harness room.

We've added a lot of straps and buckles since the days when a horse might wear just a blanket and a bit of rope for a bridle! Just what *does* the well-dressed horse wear today?

Saddle Up!

Unless you're riding bareback, the saddle is one of the first pieces of tack you'll meet. In North America, that saddle will most likely be a Western or English saddle.

If you rent a horse from a stable while on vacation and go on a trail ride, you'll probably find yourself in a Western saddle. This is the big, deep saddle with a horn that is used by

Western saddle   *English saddle*

cowboys. It was designed to be comfortable to sit in all day long while riding trails, herding cattle, and doing ranch work. The horn was—and still is—used when a rider ropes a calf or cow. You loop the rope around the saddle horn to hold on to the lassoed animal.

A Western saddle doesn't have built-in padding for the horse's back, so it is placed on top of a thick saddle blanket to cushion it. The strap that holds the saddle on the horse is called a "cinch." The cinch is fastened in place with a strap called a "latigo."

Western stirrups are often wooden with leather coverings, but they can also be made out of metal. Stirrups may also have leather hoods, called "tapaderos," attached in front to protect the rider's feet from brushing against things on a trail ride. A tapadero also stops a foot from sliding through the stirrup.

An English saddle looks quite different from a Western saddle. The first thing you'll notice is that it doesn't have a horn. This kind of saddle was designed for riding, jumping, and traveling for miles over country-side—not for roping cows.

An English saddle has built-in padding underneath to protect the horse's back. It also sits on a pad placed on the horse's back. A rectangular saddle pad is also often called a blanket. (In Great Britain, a saddle-shaped pad is called a "numnah." This term comes from a word meaning "carpet" in a language spoken in India.)

Saddle pad

An English saddle's stirrups are made of steel. They're often called "irons." A strap called a "girth" holds the English saddle in place and is fastened with buckles.

SPECIAL KINDS OF SADDLES

The basic Western and English saddles come in many other shapes and styles. The form of the saddle suits the kind of riding it'll be used for.

A Western saddle, for example, can be retooled for riding very long distances. It may have extra padding and a deeper seat. Other special Western saddles are made for rodeo events, such as reining—a sport that involves having a galloping horse slide to a sudden stop. This saddle is extra high in front.

A bucking-horse rider, however, uses a Western saddle that doesn't have a horn. Special saddles are also made for cattle roping, barrel racing, and other events.

English saddles are also redesigned for different uses. Dressage saddles, for example, are designed to help riders sit deeply, with thighs relaxed, and maintain close contact with the horse's body. Riders of Saddlebreds use flat-seated saddles with wide flaps that shield the rider from the horse's sweat; the front is also notched in a way that allows the horse's withers to move freely. The saddle helps the rider sit farther back on the horse, again to allow the horse's front legs to show off their high action.

Special saddles are also made for jumping, and others are used by police officers, military riders, and parade riders. Jockeys use very tiny saddles that are little more than holders for stirrups! These miniature saddles may weigh less than a pound (about half a kilogram).

Headgear

Horse headgear consists of halters, bridles, and bits.

bits

A halter is the basic straps-and-buckles headgear you'll see on a horse who's not tacked up for a ride. (It's also called a headcollar or a headstall.) It's used to control a horse when a person is leading or holding it. It may be made out of leather, nylon webbing, or simply rope. A lead line is attached to a ring on the halter.

halter

A bridle is much more complicated than a halter because it includes a bit, the bar that goes in a horse's mouth. A rider uses the bit to communicate with and control the horse. Most bits are made out of metal; some are rubber or plastic. Bits are designed in dozens of ways so that riders can pick just the right kind for each horse. They range from very gentle to very strong ones.

A bit is attached to the bridle by straps. Like the halter, the bridle can be made out of leather, nylon webbing, or rope. Together, bit and bridle put pressure on different parts of the horse's mouth and head when a rider handles the reins attached to the bit.

Western bosal bridle

Western ranch bridle

English bridle

The bit puts pressure on the horse's tongue and toothless parts of its gums called "bars." Different kinds of bits may also affect the horse's lips, chin, mouth corners, and the sides of its face. The bridle's noseband puts pressure on its nose, and the crownpiece puts pressure behind its ears. Some horses wear bridles without bits, called "hackamores." Hackamores work by putting pressure mainly on a horse's nose.

hackamore

Weird Gear

You may see some pretty strange stuff added to a horse's headgear.

ear net

For example, what would you make of a horse wearing a brightly colored crocheted cap on its head, with its ears stuck into little ear-shaped pockets? This horse isn't in a fashion show. It's wearing an "ear net"! An ear net helps keep pesky flies out of its ears. (It can also help dampen the sounds of a roaring crowd, a noise that can upset some show jumpers.)

Some horses may sport flat pieces of leather that sit between the bit and the reins. These are known as "slobber straps." They keep the reins out of the water when a horse drinks. They're also used to link certain kinds of reins to bits.

A horse who throws its head up may wear a strap that prevents it from lifting its head too high. This strap is called a martingale. A "standing" martingale runs from the horse's girth through its front legs to a point on its bridle's noseband. A neck strap keeps it in place around the neck. A "running" martingale is also attached to the girth, but it divides into two straps that end in rings; the reins go through these rings.

blinker hood

You may also see racehorses wearing colorful "blinker hoods" on their heads. These hoods have eyeholes that are partly covered by plastic cups. The cups stop the horse from seeing what's going on behind it or off to the sides. A trainer may put a hood on a horse to help it concentrate or keep it calm. A hood with just one cup is used on a horse that tends to run crookedly by veering off to one side.

Horses that pull carriages often have blinkers attached to their bridles. These blinkers are square pieces of leather. They're also called "blinders" or "winkers." They block the horse's rear and side vision to keep it from being distracted or alarmed.

Horseshoes

How often do you outgrow your shoes? No matter how fast your feet grow, you probably don't need new shoes every four to eight weeks (even though you might like to get new shoes at that rate!). But that's how quickly a horse may outgrow hers.

A horse's hooves grow continuously, just as your nails do. They grow at a rate of about a quarter to half an inch (5 to 10 mm) a month. As a result, they need to be trimmed and rasped down regularly. The horse's shoes, meanwhile, suffer wear and tear and need to be replaced.

The job of trimming, rasping, and fitting shoes is done by a "farrier." (You may also hear farriers called "black-

smiths." A blacksmith is a person who makes and fixes iron and steel items. In olden times, the village blacksmith often shod horses, too.)

A farrier not only needs to know how to work with metal, but also must know all about how a horse's legs work. A farrier doesn't just yank off old shoes and slap on new ones. He or she shapes shoes to fit an individual horse's hooves, trims the hooves, and fixes hoof problems, such as cracks. A farrier and a vet often work together to help a horse with an injured leg. Special shoes can also help a horse with an odd or unbalanced gait.

New Shoes

A farrier's job starts with removing the horse's old shoes. Then the soles of the horse's feet are pared—a chore that's a bit like buffing a callused foot. Next, the farrier trims and files the hooves.

The shoes, which are usually made of aluminum or steel, come next. Like shoes for people, horseshoes come in different sizes. The farrier starts with one of these basic shoes and hammers it into the right shape to fit a particular horse's hooves. He or she puts it on an anvil to hammer it.

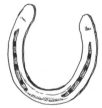

If you ever watch a horse being shod, you may see the farrier stick a shoe into a fire to heat it before hammering it. Heating the metal makes it softer so the farrier can shape it.

Then the farrier may do something that surprises you: He may stick the hot shoe on the horse's hoof! But don't worry. The horse doesn't feel a thing. The hard part of its hoof has no nerves and can't feel the heat. But the hot shoe "browns" the edge of the hoof wherever it touches. The farrier examines the mark to see where the hoof needs more trimming to make it level.

Finally, it's time to make those perfectly fitted shoes stay on the horse's feet. This is done by nailing them to the hooves. Yes, you read that right: They're nailed on. But remember—the hard part of the hoof feels no pain.

The farrier carefully pounds the nails through holes in the shoe. The points of the nails poke out of the sides of the hoof. The farrier twists off the sharp points. Then the nails are hammered so that they bend down.

Finally, the farrier rasps the hoof to make everything smooth— and the horse is good to go.

Why Horses Wear Shoes

Horses that are used for riding and driving need shoes because they often travel on hard ground, such as roads and trails. They also put lots of wear and tear on their hooves because they are carrying or pulling extra weight. As a result, their hooves wear down very quickly without horseshoes.

But shoes also stop hooves from wearing down correctly, which means they grow too long. That's why a farrier trims the hooves when fitting new shoes.

What about horses who aren't shod? Owners whose horses aren't used on rough surfaces sometimes let their horses go barefoot. There are also many horse owners who firmly believe that it's healthier for horses to go without shoes. Some barefoot horses are able to keep their hooves worn down naturally, though many still need regular trimming.

Signs and Symbols

In North America, Native Americans painted their horses' hides with symbolic designs such as lightning bolts and handprints. They still do for special events today.

You can find out more at this website:
www.nv.blm.gov/carson/KidsPage/kids_indian_horse.htm.

Choose Your Shoes!

Most horses wear the basic metal, U-shaped shoe you picture when you hear the word "horseshoe." But horseshoes also come in other styles—including high heels!

A horseshoe may be flat on the bottom, or it may be grooved so that it grips muddy or soft ground better. It may have knobs, called "studs" or "caulks," that improve the grip even more, especially on grass. The studs may be part of the shoe, or they may be special screws that can be added or removed as needed.

Some horseshoes also have a bar across the back where the opening usually is. The bar helps relieve pressure on a hurting foot. A farrier may also put a leather pad across the bottom of the foot and tuck it under the metal shoe. This helps protect the sole of a horse that has a sensitive foot.

There are also special shoes for Thoroughbred racehorses, Tennessee Walking Horses, Saddlebreds, jumpers, hunters, harness horses, reining horses, and the like, for use in competition. Many police horses wear special shoes made of rubber. These shoes grip road surfaces better than steel shoes do and help stop a police horse from slipping.

Speaking of grip and slip, there are even special horseshoe pads for use in snow—kind of like snow tires for horses!

MY PRETTY PONY!

People have enjoyed decorating horses since hitching up with them thousands of years ago. They've fashioned pretty saddles and pads as well as ornate bridles.

Arabian horses in the Middle East have been beautifully tacked up since ancient times. They used to wear colorful blankets, saddles, and bridles that were often bedecked with jewels, beads, and tassels. Today, people still decorate their Arabian horses for special occasions—and not only in the Middle East! You can see Arabians in gorgeous tack wherever they're shown.

In Europe, cart horses' harnesses have always sparkled with bits of metal. Today, you'll still see decorative harnesses on Shires, Clydesdales, and other draft horses, especially in shows.

Decorating horses continues to be popular—and fun! Some horse girls, for example, like to attach sparkly "bridle charms" to their horses' halters and bridles. The charms are usually attached on or near the brow band. And most pony camps end with a parade of horses decorated with colorful ribbons, bows, and other finery.

Horse Boots

Riders wear boots—and many horses do, too. Horse boots are designed to protect a horse's lower legs or hooves in different situations. Here are a few common kinds:

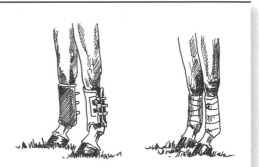

Bell boots are rubbery, cup-shaped boots that fit around the horse's front "ankles." They protect its heels and coronets from being accidentally clipped by the toes of its hind hooves when it jumps or gallops.

Brushing boots protect horses when their legs brush together when they move. The boots are padded.

Galloping boots protect the legs from cuts a horse might suffer by accidentally kicking itself with its own high-flying, fast-moving hooves. Some riders outfit their horses with galloping boots equipped with flashing lights, just for show.

Hoof boots are plastic or rubber boots that completely cover a horse's hooves—even underneath. They're used to protect injured feet or to "shoe" a barefoot horse when it goes over rough ground. A rider can also use a hoof boot as an emergency replacement for a lost shoe.

Medicine boots, made of vinyl, are like buckets for holding foot-healing medications.

Sausage boots are rubber rings that go around the horse's pasterns. A sausage ring protects the coronet, the band at the top of the hoof where it meets the leg.

Shipping boots are thick, padded boots worn by horses traveling in trailers.

Skid boots are equipped with tough patches to protect a reining horse's fetlocks from getting bruised or burned when it comes to a sliding stop. Wearing them is like putting on the horse equivalent of elbow and knee pads when you're skateboarding.

Soaking boots are basically boots with built-in buckets. They're used on horses who need to soak sore feet in water.

Splint boots protect the splint bones in the lower legs.

Sport boots (also called "tendon boots") support the tendons inside a horse's legs (just as high-topped sneakers give some extra support to your ankles). Horses wear support boots for all kinds of activities, such as barrel racing and jumping.

Leg Wraps

Have you ever seen horses with elastic bandages wrapped around their legs? These horses aren't injured. The bandages, known as leg wraps or polo wraps, help support tendons in the legs. They're like the sport bandages worn by many human athletes.

Horsey Hair Styles

Rippling manes! Flowing tails! Some breeds, such as Friesians, have beautiful, thick manes that can reach nearly to the ground. Other breeds, such as Arabians, are famous for their beautiful tails.

In everyday life, these manes and tails quickly get snarled and messy without grooming. Even a typical horse's mane and tail need a good brushing after a day in a pasture. Brushing gets rid of tangles and all the straw and other junk that gets stuck in the horse's hairs.

Simply grooming a horse usually takes care of bed-head and tangle-tail. But horses going into a show ring, a parade, or other special events often have a lot more attention lavished on their manes and tails.

The Mane Event: Braids, Bands, and Bows

A horse's mane grows along the crest of his neck, from the top of his head down to his withers. The part that hangs down on his forehead is called the forelock. The rest of the mane drapes along the neck. It may naturally lie on both sides or just the right or left.

For many breeds of horse, "going natural" is the main mane style. Arabians, Morgans, and Lipizzans all have long manes.

Other breeds' manes are cut, braided, or both. There are different traditions for each breed. Many of these traditions have practical roots. Braids on a hunter, for example, kept it clean on cross-country rides. Braiding also kept the mane from interfering with the rider's grip on the reins. That's why hunters in shows are required to have braided manes.

Here are a few of the stylin' looks that a horse may sport. Have you seen any of them on display at horse shows or rodeos?

Braided

Horses in hunter events must have their manes braided. It's traditional for the braided mane to lie on the right side of the neck. The hunter's forelock is braided, too. Riders of show jumpers may also braid their horses' manes, but it's not required. But if you're foxhunting, braid that mane— on the right!

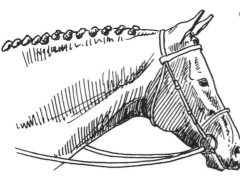

Dressage horses, too, must wear braids, and either side is okay.

Horses in saddle-seat competitions may wear a few long braids at the top of their manes, with a pretty ribbon added that goes with the rider's outfit. Their long forelocks may be braided, too.

Of course, lots of horse girls braid their horses' manes just for fun, because it looks nice.

Banded

A banded mane is a string of tiny ponytails. First, the mane is shortened. Then it is divided into fifty or so little sections. Each section is bound with a tiny rubber band. The bands are usually the same color as the mane. Banding keeps a mane flat and tidy even on a windy day. It's a favorite look for Western horses in certain events at horse shows.

Styles for guys and gals

An old tradition calls for stallions and geldings to have an odd number of braids in their manes. Mares are supposed to have an even number. Today, however, a show hunter usually sports 36 to 40 braids in its mane plus one in its forelock. A dressage horse usually wears from 16 to 21 braids.

Pulled

While it's not nice to pull someone's hair, plenty of horses have their manes pulled regularly! In this case, "pulling" means yanking out long, straggly bits of hair. Only a few hairs are yanked out at a time. Pulling thins the mane and evens the edges, creating a clean, sleek look.

Show horses with braided manes have their manes pulled. Most Thoroughbred racehorses have pulled manes, too, but it's not required.

Does pulling a mane hurt the horse? No. There aren't a lot of nerve endings in the crest, so the horse doesn't feel like you do when somebody rakes a brush through your tangled hair. That doesn't mean horses like it any more than most dogs like a bath. But every horse is different. Some horses fuss about pulling, while others couldn't care less.

Roached

A roached mane is kind of like an equine crewcut. Roaching is cutting or shaving a mane so that it's very, very short. It's a good look for a horse whose mane is naturally skimpy. Roaching (or "hogging," as it's called in the U.K.) is also done to show off the curve or strength of a horse's neck.

A polo pony's mane is roached so that it doesn't get in the way of the mallet or reins during the game. Three-gaited Saddlebreds traditionally have their manes roached (but five-gaited ones keep their long locks!).

Fancy Tails

A horse's tail is a very useful appendage. It's an excellent fly-swisher. It's a great signal flag for communicating moods to other horses (and people). It helps a horse balance as it turns while running. And it's also a fine excuse to show off some braiding!

A hunter, for example, is typically shown with the top half of its tail braided. The lower part, called the "skirt," is left free flowing. A polo pony's entire tail is braided, then folded up and taped securely (to keep it from getting caught in a swinging mallet). A racehorse's tail may be braided this way on a muddy day so that it doesn't become caked with mud.

Sometimes, you'll see a horse with a tail cut straight across at the bottom. This is called a "banged tail." Dressage horses' tails are often banged. Thoroughbred racehorses' tails sometimes are, too. Banged tails are more common in Great Britain and Ireland than in the United States.

For some breeds, however, braids and bangs are *never* in style. Arabians, Morgans, and Andalusians are some of the breeds that are always shown with their natural tails.

Phony Tails

A horse with a skimpy or short tail may be doozied up for the show ring with a "tail extension." A tail extension is a fake tail that is braided or tied into a horse's natural tail. It's usually made out of horsehair, but some tails are made out of artificial hairs. They're allowed for many breeds, such as quarter horses and paint horses. But other breed associations, such as those for Arabians and Morgans, don't allow them.

Practice Makes Perfect

Practice on a real mane and tail if you're lucky enough to have a horse (or know somebody who owns one). If you don't have access to a horse, get together with some other horse-crazy girls and practice on each other's hair! You can also try them out on toy horses that have free-flowing manes and tails.

Whisking Off Whiskers

Sometimes a horse might just get a trim to make her tidy. Perhaps she'll have the hair dangling from her fetlocks trimmed. Or maybe she'll have her ears trimmed. The long hair draping from her lower jaw may also be snipped. What about the long whiskers on a horse's muzzle and chin? Many horse owners leave these alone unless their horses are going to be in a horse show, because horses use their whiskers to feel things, just as cats do.

Clip, Clip!

In summer, a horse's coat is short and sleek. She cools off easily on a hot day by sweating. In winter, however, her coat may be thick and fuzzy. This plush winter coat keeps her warm and dry in cold, wet weather. It's so good at holding in heat that snow may even pile up on her back, because her body heat won't leak out of her coat to melt it.

So why do people sometimes clip horses in autumn to get rid of their winter coats and use blankets to keep them warm instead?

The main reason a horse owner might whip out the clippers is to keep a horse healthy if she's going to work hard in winter. A horse who works hard sweats. If her coat is long and thick, she gets hotter faster and sweats even more. (Imagine running for miles while wearing a heavy winter coat!) Plus, after she's done working, she won't dry off quickly, which means she could easily get chilled.

A horse may also be clipped if she's going to appear in shows. Clips you might commonly see include the blanket clip, the full clip, the hunter clip, the slip clip, and the trace clip.

Cozy Blankets

Clipped horses need blankets to keep them warm in winter. A winter blanket, or "rug," has an inner lining to keep the horse warm and an outer layer that blocks out wind and cold. Some blankets are waterproof. A clipped horse might also wear a lighter "exercise sheet" under his saddle if he's being taken out for a gentle ride on a winter day.

Horses may need blankets in warm weather, too. These blankets are like a windbreaker you'd wear on a spring day. They keep the horse from getting chilled if it's sweaty. A light blanket may also be put on a horse in summer to protect it from flies.

QUARTER MARKS

Have you ever seen a horse with a checkerboard, stars, diamonds, or other design on its rump? These patterns are called "quarter marks." ("Quarters" is a term for a horse's hind end.) They're created by combing the hair on the rump in different directions. A horse girl may use a stencil and hair spray in addition to a brush to style her horse's bottom in this way!

Mucky Mares and Grotty Geldings:
Or Why Horses Need Grooming

Dirt-packed hooves. Burr-choked manes. Tangled tails. Muddy legs and filthy coats. A horse can get pretty messy when he's left to his own devices. It's up to his horse girl to clean him up!

You might ask, "Why do you have to groom a horse? Wild horses get dirty and do just fine. Is it just to make them look nice?"

Grooming does make a horse look nice. A shiny coat and flowing mane and tail are pretty. But there are also more important reasons for grooming a horse.

The most important reason to clean up your horse: It helps keep him healthy. A horse's entire body should be checked every day, and combining this task with grooming makes sense. (If there isn't time for a full grooming, this daily checkup can be as simple as running your hand over the horse's entire body.)

By checking and grooming the horse daily, you can find anything different or odd that has appeared on his body: a bump, lump, scratch, sore, tick, patch of fungus (like ringworm), swelling, painful area, or overly warm spot that might be a sign of an infection or injury. You'll also notice if there's anything wrong with his feet or his shoes.

Grooming also gets rid of dirt that could be trapped under the horse's saddle, girth, or bridle and hurt her. (Parts of the horse that will be under tack should always be cleaned before riding, not only to keep him comfortable but also to prevent sores from forming.) Grooming also massages the horse's skin and muscles, which makes him feel really good.

Plus, grooming is a nice way to bond with a horse. Horses naturally groom their friends with their teeth, and scientists have found it even lowers their blood pressure. What better way to convince a horse that you're his pal!

Sophie Says: I'm a horse-crazy girl! Many people wonder why we put up with mucking, but we horse girls know that it is only one small favor to your horse—to give it a nice place to live. And it's especially rewarding when the horse you adore recognizes you and canters across the paddock to greet you!

You Scratch My Back . . .

If you watch horses, chances are you'll see at least two of them pair up to groom each other. The duo will stand side by side, nose to tail. Then, each horse will nibble the other's neck, back, and withers. This not only helps horses groom places that are hard for them to reach, but also helps them bond with each other. Mutual grooming is so soothing to a horse that its heart rate even drops. If you ever groom a horse, it may nibble you to return the favor!

Grooming Tools

Body brush: a soft brush for brushing the horse's body to get rid of dirt and shed hair

Dandy brush: a stiff brush for removing dried-on mud

Face brush: An ultra soft brush for brushing the horse's face

Hoof pick: a tool with a blunt metal hook on one end for cleaning out the horse's hooves; it may also have bristles for brushing out dirt

Mane comb: a wide-toothed comb for use on a horse's mane as well as its tail. It's useful if you're going to braid or thin the hairs.

Metal curry comb: a metal comb used for cleaning out a body brush

Plastic or rubber curry comb: a comb for cleaning dirt from the body and legs

Rubber grooming mitt: a flexible rubber "mitten" covered with tiny bumps; it can be used like a body brush to remove dirt from the coat, or as a scrubber when shampooing a horse

Shedding blade: a sweat scraper with metal teeth used to collect and remove shedding hair from the horse's coat; also called a shedding tool

Sponge: used to clean the horse's eyes, lips, and nostrils; a separate sponge is used to clean the horse's backside

Stable rubber: a cloth for polishing the horse's coat

Sweat scraper: a rubber blade, kind of like a windshield wiper, for scraping water off the horse's body after a bath

Water brush: a soft brush for dampening the mane and tail

All Clean and Shiny!

After a good grooming, a horse fairly gleams. The girl groom, however, is another story! She's covered with horsehair sticking to her clothes. She's got mud on her boots and pants, and probably on her face, too, where she wiped away sweat with her forearm. She looks like she could use a session with a giant-sized lint brush. But she's probably still got a stall to muck and tack to clean. After everything's done, however, a good old-fashioned bath or shower and a spin in the washing machine (*for her clothes!*) puts a shine back on her, too.

Clothes-Horses II

Rider Attire

If you go on a trail ride while on vacation, you'll see people wearing all kinds of clothing on horseback—and most of it will be wrong, wrong, wrong! That's because most people decide to ride on the spur of the moment, just for fun—which is why you'll see sneakers, sandals, and maybe even flip-flops in the stirrups!

But if you plan to ride, it's a good idea to dress properly. You can't go wrong in a pair of jeans and smooth-soled boots—and not because it's "fashionable." Riding attire is what it is because it's practical and safe.

On Your Feet

Both English and Western riders, for example, wear smooth-soled boots with a low heel. Why smooth? Because a bumpy sole could get stuck in the stirrup. Why the heel? Because without it, your foot could slide right through the stirrup, which could get stuck looped around your heel or ankle.

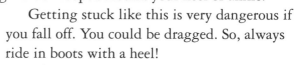

Getting stuck like this is very dangerous if you fall off. You could be dragged. So, always ride in boots with a heel!

A boot also protects your foot if the horse steps on it. It's no fun when a hard-hoofed animal weighing about 1,000 pounds (450 kg) plants his metal-shod foot on your toe even when you *are* wearing boots. Imagine how painful this would be if you were wearing sneakers!

English riders may wear ankle-high boots called "paddock boots" or "jodhpur boots." Or they can opt for "riding tennies," boots that look a little like tennis shoes. Heels on English boots are less than an inch (2.5 cm) tall. If you take riding lessons, you'll probably be asked to show up in boots with a half-inch (1.2 cm) heel.

Western riders wear "cowboy boots." This kind of boot has a pointy toe. Some cowboy boots have low heels, but others have heels as high as 2 inches (5 cm). Why so high? Because Western stirrups don't automatically break away from the saddle if the rider falls off with a foot stuck in a stirrup as many English stirrups are designed to do. A tall heel, however, prevents the

Well-Heeled Boots

Some English and Western riders wear metal devices on their boots called "spurs." The spurs extend a rider's reach and help her touch her horse's flanks.  Riding with spurs takes practice, however, because a little spur goes a long way. In general, only experienced riders should use them.

foot from slipping through the stirrup and getting stuck in the first place.

Jeans and Jodhs

Jeans are decent pants to wear for riding. After all, they're the trousers of choice for cowpokes!
So why are there all these special fancy pants for riding?

The answer can be summed up in one word: chafing. Just as ill-fitting shoes will give you a blister on your heel, pants with seams or folds that rub while you ride will irritate your legs. Even comfy denim jeans may have bumpy seams and can leave you saddle-sore.

That's one reason why people devised special pants for riding. The seams, for example, are on the outside of the leg, not the inside, so they don't rub while riding. The inner legs have tough pads that give extra grip. The material is tight-fitting and flexible, so the rider can feel the horse and move freely without any fabric bunching up.

For English riders, "riding pants" are breeches or jodhpurs ("jodhs" for short). Breeches fit tightly, come partway down the lower leg, and are worn with tall boots. Jodhpurs fit a little more loosely, reach down to the ankle, and are worn with shorter boots.

Western riders still favor jeans, but they also have other choices. There are denim riding jeans that are made with stretchy fabric, and breeches made for long-distance endurance riding.

People who ride in shows wear clothes made for these events. English riders who do dressage wear long coats and top hats. Western riders may wear flashy shirts decked out with sparkly rhinestones. But everyday riding clothes are more casual.

"Breeches and Cream"

Traditional English riding wear has typically been "breeches and cream"— that is, cream-colored breeches. This is still a favorite color, even for everyday riding. But today you can buy breeches and jodhs in almost every color. You can even choose patterns, including leopard spots and flowers, if you like!

Use Your Head—Wear a Helmet!

It can't be said often enough—never ride without a helmet! A helmet absorbs the shock of a fall or a kick. *Without a helmet, it's your brain that absorbs the shock instead.* Wearing a helmet can help prevent a brain injury or death due to such an injury.

Most riding schools and horse camps won't even let you near their horses unless you're wearing a helmet. While you can hurt your head falling off a horse, you can also be hit in the head while on the ground by a rearing, kicking, or otherwise misbehaving horse.

Since 1990, riding helmets have been designed to meet high standards set by a group called the American Society of Testing Materials—ASTM for short. Another abbreviation you'll see is SEI, which stands for Safety Equipment Institute. This organization also tests equipment to make sure that it's as safe as can be.

You can go online to check out which equestrian helmets are on their list at **www.seinet.org** (use their "search" feature to find the list). At this time, helmets by GPA are considered the best.

Caution! Lots of people think it's okay to wear a bike helmet when they ride a horse. (Luckily, trail-ride wranglers and riding instructors know better, and stop them!) A bike helmet and a riding helmet *do not* work the same way. They are each designed to protect the head from injuries linked specifically to biking or horseback riding because each activity has its own dangers.

Helmets by Design

English riding events call for traditional black or dark-gray helmets in the ring. But when you're just riding for fun or schooling a horse, you can doozy up your helmet any way you like. Lots of girls choose a colorful helmet or decorate a traditional one with a snazzy helmet cover. Some girls add stickers or draw on their helmets.

Other Bits and Pieces ...

Here are a few other items of clothing you may see on riders—or on you, if you take up riding. If you take up dressage, polo, the sidesaddle, or foxhunting, you'll need to learn about different dress codes as well as items of clothing. And it's not only English riders who have rules to follow—Western riders do, too. In some kinds of shows, they even have to wear outfits tailored to the breed of horse they're riding!

Chaps: These are leather leg coverings worn by Western riders over their jeans. Chaps help a rider grip the saddle and protect against rubbing. They also protect the legs from bushes and cactuses out on the trail.

English riders may also wear chaps for extra grip, protection, and, in winter, warmth. Chaps that cover the whole leg are called full chaps. Half-chaps are just that—chaps that go from ankle to knee.

In shows, parades, and rodeos, Western chaps may be fringed and fancy. Chaps often match the color of a cowgirl's pants. In fact, she may opt to wear the same color from head to toe—hat and boots included!

Gloves: A rider may wear gloves for the same reason anybody does—to keep her hands warm! But gloves are also good for gripping. Reins don't slip out of hands quite so easily. Some gloves have pebbly or rough undersides to help improve grip. A rider who enters shows will also have special "dress" gloves for these events.

Western gloves for shows and parades are often decked out with fancy fringe dangling from the wrists. For everyday riding, a Western rider may wear tough gloves, the kind built for working with ropes and calves.

Bling in the Ring!

English riding attire got its start in Great Britain, but it's worn all around the world today wherever people use English saddles. It's traditional and conservative, and it's still the standard for modern equestrian sports such as dressage, show jumping, and saddle-seat riding. It's what riders wear in equestrian events in the Olympics.

Western riding attire in the show ring is based on traditional clothing, too—but in this case, the attire is cowboy duds. Riders in events such as roping competitions wear basic gear that looks nice but lets them work freely. In other events, cowgirls can wear brightly colored shirts that sparkle with rhinestones, crystals, sequins, and glitter.

Other hot-to-trot fashions are a jacket or a vest with a stretchy knit shirt called a "slinky." A cowgirl can also pick colors that go well with her horse and coordinate her saddle pad with her outfit.

Safety vest:

Some riders choose to wear safety vests that protect the upper body in a fall. These vests can be worn under regular clothes. They're required in some equestrian sports. Riders in eventing, for example, must wear them during the cross-country part of the competition. Jockeys, polo players, bronc riders, and others wear them, too. (Safety vests are also called body protectors—for good reason!)

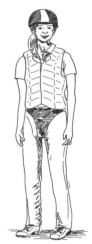

Shirts:

A rider's shirt may be extra fancy if she's in a show. A girl riding in English riding events, for example, may wear a tidy shirt with a standup collar and a funny name: "ratcatcher"! With the shirt, she may wear a "stock tie"—a white piece of fabric tied around her neck and fastened in place with a pin.

A stock is usually reserved for formal equestrian events, such as jumper stake classes, dressage, or foxhunting. It harks back to foxhunting attire. A stock not only made a rider look neat but also served as a useful tool in emergencies. It could be used as a bandage on an injured hound, horse, or rider, or as a sling for a broken arm. A rider could also use it to replace a broken rein. (A cowgirl's bandanna can do these jobs, too—and is also mighty useful for covering your nose and mouth when the riding gets dusty!)

Today, English riders usually wear monogrammed collars instead—that is, collars with a rider's initials embroidered on them.

Who's the Odd Girl Out?

Riding clothes can look stylish—but what's most important is that they provide both comfort and safety.

Creativity at Play

Many horse-crazy girls combine their love for horses with their creativity. Here are a few fun ideas.

Equine Collage

Look for pictures of horses and horsey items in magazines and catalogs. Cut them out and use them to make a collage for your bedroom door. Look for words in the headlines that you can string together to sum up your thoughts and feelings about horses. This is a great use for old tack catalogs.

Stampin' Stampede

Use stamps of horses to make your own stationery. (You can find horse stamps at craft and toy stores.) Fold a sheet of paper in half, then fold it in half again to make a card, then stamp. If you have card-size envelopes, stamp them, too. You can also stamp Kraft paper or paper grocery bags to make wrapping paper.

Tack Time

Try making some tack for your model horses.

Cut blankets out of scraps of fabric. Trim the edges by gluing on rickrack, seam binding, or bias tape. You can also trim with fabric scraps.

Cut saddles out of felt. If you can score vinyl fabric samples, these make great saddles, too.

Use yarn, string, leather laces, and the like to make bridles and halters.

Carousel Horses

Have you ever hopped aboard a horse on a carousel? If so, you probably picked the horse you wanted to ride as you waited for your turn. Maybe you chose a really beautiful one with flowers in its mane and tail. Let your imagination go for a spin and design your own carousel horse.

Draw a horse with the most dazzling, ornate saddle and bridle you can think of. Festoon its mane and tail with stars, flowers, and ribbons. You can even cut out fabric and glue it on, or use glitter glue, sequins, and stickers. Then, cut out your horse. Tape it to a drinking straw, which makes a super carousel pole. Stand it upright in a blob of modeling clay embedded in a cup, a small flowerpot, or the like. (Need inspiration? Check out photos on the site of the National Carousel Association at www.nca-usa.org.)

Horse Sports

Here are some of the many activities and events enjoyed by horses and horse people.

Hacking

"Hacking" is what you probably dream about when you think about going horseback riding. It's simply getting on a horse and riding for fun—on a trail, a bridle path, a beach, or the like. Some people prefer to ride alone; others like to ride with friends. Riding schools may take classes on hacks, too. Even racehorses and show horses get breaks from their training schedules and go out for nice, relaxing rides.

Showing

At horse shows, horses can be shown "in hand," meaning that they're led by a halter or bridle with their handlers walking beside them. These classes are either breeding classes, in which the conformation and quality of the horse is judged, or "showmanship," in which the handler's preparation and handling of the horse is judged.

A horse shown in hand gets a close look from a judge. The owner is expected to groom the horse beautifully, and the horse should be calm and content in line. The judge will want to see the horse walk and trot, too.

In a showing class for riders, the judge watches as competitors walk, trot, and canter. Riders may also be asked to back their horses, dismount and untack them, or perform other "tests," as requested by the judge.

Both English and Western riders have these kinds of showing classes. One popular Western class is called "Western Pleasure," in which the horse is judged on just how pleasant he is to ride. A horse that wins this class is a great choice to take on a trail ride.

Playing Mounted Games!

Ever play freeze tag on horseback? How about musical chairs? These are just some of the games you might play in a "gymkhana," a horse show that includes these mounted games and often other events such as jumping or showing. It's often a local event geared for young riders. (See page 92.)

Dressage

"Dressage" comes from a French word that means "to train." But when you see a dressage horse and rider in action, you're more likely to think it means "to dance."

Dressage is the art of training a horse to move naturally and easily, in a beautifully balanced way. The horse moves gracefully from one motion to the next, following his rider's slightest command in such a calm and obedient way that you can't even see the rider's cues.

In a dressage test, horse and rider perform a set series of gaits and movements and are judged on how well they do them. Find out more about dressage online at these websites:

United States Dressage Federation: www.usdf.org

Dressage Canada: www.dressagecanada.org

Show Jumping

A horse and rider in a show-jumping competition leap over a series of jumps in a certain order. The goal is to jump cleanly without knocking down the poles. The course must also be done quickly, because horse and rider are also racing against the clock!

The lowest score wins, so the rider tries to avoid piling up points called "faults." Faults are given for knocking a pole off a jump, going over the time limit, or refusing a jump.

Hunter Jumping

Like a show jumper, a show hunter leaps over jumps. Unlike a show jumper, a hunter and her rider are judged on how they *look* going over the jumps. A show jumper can pop over the jumps like a kangaroo and win, as long as she goes clean and fast. But a hunter, like a dressage horse, is expected to show the right style as she goes along. The rider also has to wear certain kinds of clothes, and the horse's mane and tail are braided for top-rated shows.

Cross-country

As you might guess, cross-country is riding across the countryside and jumping obstacles along the way. The obstacles are things you'd find in the countryside, such as gates, ditches, banks, and logs.

Three-Day Eventing

In eventing, a horse and rider compete in three sports in one! They do dressage, show jumping, and cross-country. The three events are often spread across three days. You can learn more about this sport by visiting the website of the Rolex Kentucky Three-Day Event: www.rk3de.org. More info can also be found on the website of the Badminton Horse Trials in Great Britain: www.badminton-horse.co.uk. And you can watch *The Little Horse That Could*, a documentary about a hardworking little Connemara stallion named Erin Go Bragh, who became a great event horse.

horsing around

Mounted games are lots of fun! They're also a great way to practice your riding skills, improve your balance, and give a boost to your ability to communicate with your horse or pony. Many riding schools include them as part of lessons. You can also participate in games at gymkhanas and in Pony Club events. There are games designed for individuals, pairs, and teams.

Bending Race: pony and rider weave around poles at a gallop, without knocking the poles over

Balloon Bursting Race: riders take turns dashing across the field, with each rider on a team using a stick to pop a balloon along the way

Egg and Spoon Race: a bending race done while carrying an egg in a metal spoon without dropping or breaking it!

Sack Race: riders hop along in sacks while leading ponies (who don't wear sacks!)

Stepping-Stone Race: riders walk on a series of "stepping-stones" (such as upside-down flowerpots) while leading ponies, then jump onto their ponies' backs and race to the finish line

Endurance Riding

Slow and steady wins the race—or at least crosses the finish line! The motto of endurance riding is "To finish is to win."

Endurance rides test how fit a horse is to travel long distances. A long endurance ride may be 100 miles (160 km) long or even more. Horse and rider must complete the ride in a certain amount of time. Along the way, there are vet checks to make sure the horses are doing okay. If they are not, they are "pulled" from the event.

Being first to cross the finish line doesn't mean you're the winner, though! If you ride too hard and your poor horse arrives with his tongue hanging out, forget it. It's the first horse to finish the distance and pass the final vet check who'll get the honors. Another honor is receiving the "Best Conditioned" award. This honor is not an instant award for the winner—it can go to another horse whose fitness is tip-top.

Driving

Harness horses and their drivers compete in the show ring, too. In a pleasure-driving class, a horse may be judged on how well it goes and the driver on how well she drives. A class might include obstacles, such as traffic cones, to drive around at a quick pace.

Drivers compete in cross-country events, too. There aren't any jumps to go over, but there *are* obstacles like bridges and water crossings. Drivers also compete in an international discipline called combined driving, which is a lot like three-day eventing, but for drivers. Contested over three days, it consists of dressage, marathon (cross-country), and obstacles.

Find out more about driving horses at the website of the American Driving Society: www.americandrivingsociety.org.

Rodeo

A rodeo is a test of a Western horse and his rider's skill. Rodeo events have their roots in real jobs done on ranches in both the past and the present. Some events, such as calf-roping, focus on how a horse and its rider work together when dealing with cattle. Others focus on just the horse and rider.

There are two types of rodeo events: "roughstock" and "timed." Roughstock consist of bareback riding, saddle bronc riding, and bull riding. The contestant's score depends on his performance as well as the animal's. Timed events include steer wrestling, team roping, barrel racing, and steer roping.

Polo

Polo is a little like field hockey on horseback. It pits two teams of horses and riders against each other. Riders use sticks called "mallets" to whack a ball into the opposing team's goal. The horses are called "polo ponies." Periods of play are called "chukkers."

Horseball

Horseball is sort of like basketball on horseback. The ball used in this game has leather loops attached to it so that riders can grab it without having to let go of their reins. It's tossed from rider to rider as the team tries to throw the ball through into the opposing team's hoop.

Flat Racing

Speed, speed, and more speed! Flat racing—in which Thoroughbred race-horses run over flat ground and don't jump over anything—is all about crossing the finish line first. But there is also strategy involved.

A jockey must carefully control a racehorse to make its energy last. He or she may urge the horse to run at the front of the pack or to find a place in the middle. The jockey also holds the horse back to keep it from using up all its speed at the wrong time, and gets it to unleash its speed at just the right moment.

A Day at the Races

The most famous horse race in the United States is the Kentucky Derby. The Derby is run at a track called Churchill Downs in Kentucky on the first Saturday in May. It's 1 1/4 miles (2 km) long.

The Derby is part of a three-race series called the Triple Crown. The other two races are the Preakness Stakes and the Belmont Stakes. The Preakness is run on the third Saturday in May at Pimlico Race Course in Maryland. The Belmont Stakes is run three weeks later, in June, at Belmont Park in New York.

Harness Racing

A horse in a harness race pulls a lightweight, two-wheeled cart called a "sulky." And he doesn't gallop. Harness races are for Standardbreds, which are either trotters or pacers, not both. Find out more about harness racing online at the website of the U.S. Trotting Association, which has a harness-racing magazine for kids. (You can write for a free copy.) See for yourself at www.hoofbeatsmagazine.com/youthbeats/main.cfm.

Steeplechase Race

A steeplechase is a flat race that includes big jumps. The most famous steeplechase is England's Grand National, in which horses face thirty fences! The most famous National winner was a bay gelding named Red Rum. Red Rum is the only horse to have won the National three times (in 1973, 1974, and 1977). Find out more about the National online at www.grand-national-world.co.uk/gnw/the_race/history.html.

A HORSE OF CERTAIN COLORS

Jockeys wear colorful riding outfits called "silks." Every owner has a one-of-a-kind combination of colors and patterns, so you can tell at a glance who owns what horse. Want to make up your own silks? Visit www.jockeyclub.com/silks.asp and open the link for "application for silks registration." Print out the application, then fill it out and color it in with your dream silks, just for fun. (But do NOT actually send it in!)

You Go, Girl!

On May 16, 2009, a tall, graceful bay filly named Rachel Alexandra galloped into history at Pimlico Race Course. That's the day she romped to victory in the Preakness Stakes—the first filly to win this race since 1924. She also proved that she could run against the year's best colts and win.

The beautiful filly also blew away the year's best fillies in races for "girls" only: She won the Kentucky Oaks by 20 1/4 lengths, and the Mother Goose Stakes by 19 1/4 lengths! She set stakes records in some of those races and nearly broke a track record set by Secretariat at Belmont Park in 1973.

Barbaro's Story

The beautiful bay Thoroughbred race-horse Barbaro won six of six races in 2005 and 2006. But in his seventh, the Preakness, he won the hearts of many people. Barbaro broke his leg in that race, and his owners and a team of doctors did everything they could to save him.

The three-year-old horse lived for another eight months with his leg in a cast. Many people were riveted by the story of his recovery and care. But although Barbaro's bones healed, a hoof disease called laminitis spoiled his chance for a recovery. He was humanely put to sleep in January 2007.

A memorial fund to raise money for research on horse diseases was set up in his honor. What scientists may learn from this research will help other horses in the future.

You can read about the Barbaro Memorial Fund and the story of his care online at ntra.com/content.aspx?type=other&id=17982.

History-Making Horses

Many racehorses go to live on breeding farms when they retire. They become the fathers and mothers (or "sires and dams," in horse talk) of new crops of baby racehorses. And just a handful of them arrive at the Hall of Champions at the Kentucky Horse Park after their breeding careers are finished! This website will tell you about who's living there now: www.kyhorsepark.com/kids/sub.php?pageid=16&sectionid=1.

Top Ten Famous Racehorses
(since 1900, in North America)

Every racehorse has a story. And every racehorse has his or her fans. So if your favorite racehorse isn't on this list, you can make up your own Top Ten list of Thoroughbreds. (And the horses who never become champions are still hard-working athletes who deserve respect, too.)

Our Top Ten list is made up of ten horses we think any horse girl might like to know about. Some of them are Triple Crown winners—that is, they won the Kentucky Derby, the Preakness, and the Belmont Stakes. Others are known for their winning streaks or record-setting runs.

Man o' War raced from 1919 to 1920. This big chestnut colt won 20 out of 21 races. He once came in first by 100 lengths! (A "length" is the length of a horse's body from nose to rump. You could have fit 100 horses between Man o' War and the second-place horse!)

Seabiscuit raced from 1935 to 1950. The tough little bay colt got off to a slow start in his first year, but then started winning races and breaking records. He even beat Triple Crown winner War Admiral in a two-horse race (known as a match race).

Citation raced in 1947 and 1948, took a year off, then raced again in 1950 and 1951. This bay colt won 32 of 45 races, including the Triple Crown. He was so fast that nobody ran against him in one of his races!

Northern Dancer raced from 1963 to 1964. The bay colt was the first Canadian horse to win the Kentucky Derby. He won 14 of his 18 races. (His dad, Native Dancer, won 22 out of 23!)

Secretariat raced from 1972 to 1973. The flashy chestnut colt won 16 of 21 races, including the Triple Crown. He won the Belmont by 31 lengths in world-record time!

Affirmed raced from 1977 to 1979. He won 22 of 29 races, including the Triple Crown. The chestnut colt is famous for his rivalry with another top horse, Alydar, who finished second in each Triple Crown race.

Ruffian raced from 1974 to 1975. The big, powerful, nearly-black filly won 10 out of 10 races with sizzling speed. Tragically, she broke her leg in a match race with Kentucky Derby winner Foolish Pleasure and was euthanized.

Seattle Slew raced from 1976 to 1978. He was the first horse to win the Kentucky Derby with a perfect winning streak. He won the Triple Crown and beat Triple Crown winner Affirmed in a race in 1978.

Genuine Risk raced from 1979 to 1981. The tough chestnut filly was only the second "girl" to win the Kentucky Derby. She came in second in both the Preakness and the Belmont.

Cigar raced from 1993 to 1996. During that time, the dark-bay colt won 16 races in a row! In total, he took first place in 19 of 33 races. He was Horse of the Year twice.

That's (Horse) Entertainment

Great Movies

In the early days of movies, horses were big stars. Many horses got top billing right alongside actors and actresses. Horses even made movie history by starring in the very first motion pictures ever made!

Hi, Ho, Silver Screen!

As you might guess, many movies with horses in them are Westerns—action-packed stories that take place in the western United States and are filled with runaway stagecoaches, brave cowboys, longhorn steers, and gunfights. Hundreds upon hundreds of Westerns have been made.

Many a horse, of course, appeared in a Western just to tote a cowboy or Indian around. But some horses were every bit as popular as their riders, and directors wouldn't dream of leaving these steeds out of their scripts. These horses are forever linked with their cowboy costars. After all, what good is The Lone Ranger without Silver, or Roy Rogers without Trigger?

Cue the Horses!

Horses had a rough time in the early days of the movies. They were tripped on purpose to make them fall down. Over time, laws were passed to protect animals used in movies. Trainers learned to teach horses to fall down safely on cue. And when you see horses fighting in movies, don't worry! They're wearing rubber shoes and soft coverings on their teeth so that the kicks and bites don't hurt. Today's moviemakers also make fake mechanical horses to use in really dangerous scenes.

TOP TEN HORSE MOVIES

There are lots of horse movies that aren't Westerns, of course. In these movies, horses take on starring roles as mustangs, racehorses, show horses, pets, and friends. Here, in order of their production, are ten that ended up in our winner's circle!

Rating Guide:

^ = one ear pricked; this movie's really good

^^ = two ears pricked; this movie's great

^^ ~ = two ears pricked and a tail switch; this movie's excellent!

National Velvet (1944) ^

An oldie but a goodie! A girl named Velvet Brown wins a badly behaved horse in a raffle and conspires to race him in a world-famous race called the Grand National. Velvet's so horse-crazy, you'd need to invent a whole new word for her condition! The horse, Pirate ("Pie" for short), was played by a strapping chestnut Thoroughbred named King Charles. (In the book, The Pie is a piebald.) The lucky girl who played Velvet got King Charles as a gift after filming was wrapped up. Read more about the book that inspired the movie in the Top Ten Classic Horse Books section.

Ride a Wild Pony (1975) ^^

Taff is a cream-colored Welsh pony who belongs to a poor boy named Scotty. Or does he? Is he actually a pony named Bo who belongs to a rich girl named Josie, whom Bo pulls in a wagon because Josie lost the ability to walk after suffering from polio? Without Taff, Scotty can't get to school—Taff is also his best buddy. Without Bo, Josie loses her independence and a pet she adores. You'll feel for both of them in the struggle to determine who owns the pony. This movie is hard to find but well worth tracking down. So's the book it's based on: A Sporting Proposition by James Aldridge.

The Black Stallion (1979) ^^~

Horse movies just don't come any better than this. A beautiful black Arabian stallion, called simply The Black, survives a shipwreck and being stranded on a remote island with a boy named Alec. The two form a rock-solid bond and go on to new adventures after being rescued. The Black is played by Cass Ole, a beautiful Arabian who'd been a champion show horse. He had four white socks and a blaze that were dyed black for the film. His stunt doubles included sorrel and white horses who had to be dyed completely black. (There was a follow-up film called The Black Stallion Returns, which many viewers found disappointing—it wasn't as magical as the first film, and Alec was a bit of a whiner.) Check out the book on page 104.

(continued)

Into the West (1993) ^^~

Two Irish boys are swept away from their grim city surroundings by a beautiful white horse called Tír na nÓg, who takes them on a cross-country trek. Their grandpa senses that the stallion is no ordinary horse—and he's right: Tír na nÓg has leapt out of ancient Irish legends. Three horses—a Lipizzan and two Andalusians—take turns playing the role. Their acting jobs called for everything from running on a beach to riding in an elevator. A funny, sad, exciting, beautiful movie.

The Silver Stallion (1993) ^^~

A splendid cream-colored stallion with a silver mane and tail fights to keep his herd and his freedom in the mountains of Australia, where wild horses called "brumbies" roam. He is relentlessly tracked by a man determined to make the stallion, Thowra, his own. A girl named Indi follows the story, which is told by her mom. It's based on the Silver Brumby book series written by Elyne Mitchell.

Black Beauty (1994) ^^~

There's more than one movie based on Anna Sewell's book *Black Beauty*, but this is the only one that sticks close to the story. It also tells the tale from Beauty's point of view, just like the book. In the film, we can hear Beauty's thoughts as voiced by a narrator. There are stunning scenes of horses at play and at work. Beauty is played by a black quarter horse stallion called Doc's Keepin' Time (nickname: Justin). Ginger is played by two horses—a chestnut Thoroughbred mare named Rat and a chestnut quarter horse gelding named Hightower.

Running Free (2000) ^

A chestnut foal is born on board a ship as it travels from Germany to South Africa in 1914. Upon landing, the foal is separated from his mom. An orphan stableboy befriends him and names him Lucky. The movie follows Lucky as he grows up and makes a life for himself in the desert. About ten foals played Lucky as a youngster, and a part-Saddlebred named Aladdin played him as a stallion. His archenemy is a big Friesian named Caesar.

The Young Black Stallion (2003) ^^

In this prequel to *The Black Stallion*, a young girl named Neera befriends a wild black Arabian colt in a North African desert. After a long separation, the two come together again and compete in a horse race that will spell life or death for her family's stable. The horses and scenery are gorgeous. The black horse, Shetan, is played by nine different horses, but the lead steed was a horse named Thee Cyclone—a bay who was dyed black to fit the role. Cyclone's main understudy was not only bay—but also a mare!

Dreamer (2005) ^^~

Dakota Fanning plays Cale, a girl who helps a Thoroughbred filly named Soñador recover from a broken leg. Soñador is played by a number of horses, but the story itself was inspired by one real horse—Mariah's Storm, a filly who broke her leg while racing in 1993. Amazingly, and with lots of care, Mariah's Storm recovered and returned to the track. This film has exciting racing scenes as well as quiet moments of friendship between Soñador and Cale. Wouldn't you love to have a horse who eats Popsicles and follows you around like a puppy?

Moondance Alexander (2007) ^

Moondance is a girl who's snubbed by other girls and has no friends—until she meets a spunky piebald horse with the unfortunate name of Tinkerbell. She renames him Checkers, then meets his cantankerous owner and gets a job working in a stable in return for learning to ride. Together, she and Checkers compete in a horse show, braving the contempt of judges and riders who think a pinto has no place in the show ring. Checkers was played by three different horses.

Horse Movie Runners-Up!

Can't resist adding a few also-rans!

Misty (1961)^ —Easy to find, a nice adaptation of the book *Misty of Chincoteague* by Marguerite Henry.

Phar Lap (1983) ^^~ —A stunning film that tells the true story of a great Australian racehorse. It's an also-ran only because, to date, it hasn't been released as a video or DVD that can play on machines in North America.

Smoky (1946) ^ —The story of a wild horse's ups and downs as a cow pony and bucking bronco, based on the book *Smoky* by Will James. Another version was made twenty years later in 1966.

Sophie Says:
Into the West: I really, really, *really* enjoyed this movie. There were lots of beautiful and funny horse scenes, too. ***The Silver Stallion:*** A lovely movie that shows what life is like for wild horses. ***Black Beauty:*** A one-of-a-kind movie. It's amazing how you actually know what Black Beauty is thinking. ***Dreamer:*** A great movie about a truly brave horse trying to recover from a terrible accident.

Spirit

Spirit: Stallion of the Cimarron was the first cartoon, or "animated," feature film with a horse as its main character. It tells the story of a mustang named Spirit and his battle to run free in the American West. It was released in 2002. The sounds made by the horses in the film were all made by real horses. They were recorded at a stable.

Horsey TV

Horses have been as much of a hit on TV screens as they are on the big screen. They've played lead roles in shows like *The Lone Ranger*, in which steeds Silver and Scout were as important as their riders. In shows such as *Bonanza* and other Westerns, the horses were mainly just transportation, but they added plenty of color and action.

Some horses, however, even got their own TV series—a dream come true for horse-crazy girls!

Painting Paints

Early moviemakers weren't keen on using spotted horses in their films. They preferred solid-colored brown, black, or white horses. The reason was simple: It was easy to swap one solid-colored horse for another while filming a movie. It was harder to find a double for a pinto or a horse with a funny blaze or vivid stockings.

A director might have to swap horses because one horse needed a rest. A solid-colored horse could also play more than one part. It could be a cow horse in one scene and a cart horse in another, and nobody would notice. This would be harder to do with a leopard Appaloosa!

But if necessary, a director could have a horse painted to be the right color. A famous horse like Trigger, for example, had "doubles" who took his place in some scenes or who did stunts that the star horse didn't do. The doubles had to be made up so that they looked like the star.

Oh, Wilburrrr . . .

Mister Ed was a talking horse who lived with a bumbling architect named Wilbur Post. He only talked to Wilbur, which of course made Wilbur look pretty foolish in front of other people when he insisted that Ed had told him something.

Ed was played by a palomino gelding named Bamboo Harvester. This horse had gotten his start in showbiz by performing as a parade horse as well as a show horse. He was a quick learner who could untie knots and answer a telephone. He also patiently endured wearing costumes.

To make it look as if Ed were talking, his trainer encouraged him to wiggle his lips. The horse wore a thin, clear thread—kind of like fishing line—under his upper lip. The thread was attached to his halter. His trainer signaled him to talk by tugging lightly on the line.

Mister Ed began in 1961 and ended in 1966 but was shown in repeats for many years after that. It still pops up sometimes on channels such as TV Land and Nick at Nite. Many episodes are also available on DVD.

More Black Stallions

You had to look a little harder to find horses on TV in the 1970s—but if you did, you were rewarded by the discovery of a fantastic series called *The Adventures of Black Beauty*.

This series told the story of a girl named Jenny and a stallion named Black Beauty, in England. It thrilled horse girls from 1972 to 1974. Another series, *The New Adventures of Black Beauty*, took the story to New Zealand, with Jenny as a grown-up watching her stepdaughter Vicki bond with another black stallion.

(Both series can be found on DVD now.)

In 1990, TV time was devoted to yet another black stallion—*The* Black Stallion. Walter Farley's famous Black Stallion book inspired this series, which was called *The Adventures of the Black Stallion*. It was filmed mainly in Canada and ran through 1993. You can find it on DVD today.

Pony Partners

Since 2001, horse-crazy girls have enjoyed a TV show made just for them: *The Saddle Club,* a series based on the best-selling books by Bonnie Bryant.

It follows the adventures of Carole, Stevie, and Lisa as they learn to ride and care for horses at a stable called Pine Hollow—all while enduring the scorn of arch-enemy Veronica, who refuses to care for her own horse. They also cope with other problems that crop up at the stable and among its cast of characters.

There have been three seasons of this show over the years, with new actors and actresses each time. The third season got underway in 2008. Shows are filmed in Australia. You can catch it on channels such as Discovery Kids. Older episodes are also available on DVD. And you can read about the ponies and people in the show online at **www.saddleclubtv.com**.

All Horses, All the Time

Today's horse girls can enjoy horse shows on TV 24/7! There are cable TV channels devoted entirely to horses, such as Horse TV. You can visit this channel online, too, at **www.horsetv.com**.

Horse Tales

You could probably read nothing but horse books for the rest of your life—and never read the same book twice! But of course you'll want to read the best of them.

Top Ten Classic Horse Stories

Rating Guide:

^ = one ear pricked; this book's really good

^^ = two ears pricked; this book's great

^^ ~ = two ears pricked and a tail switch; this book's excellent!

Black Beauty by Anna Sewell (1877) ^^~

The horse book that started it all! This story is told from the point of view of Black Beauty, beginning with his happy days as a colt and ending with his final home. His life is filled with highs and lows, and along the way he meets people who treat horses kindly, as well as people who are harsh and cruel.

> Anna Sewell's book *Black Beauty* was published in 1877. Anna was never a rider—she injured her ankles badly as a teenager and could barely walk after that, let alone ride. But as a passenger in carriages, she grew to love the horses that pulled them.

The book helped pave the way to better treatment of horses and other animals.

Easy to find? Yes, in both bookstores and libraries.

The Black Stallion by Walter Farley (1941) ^^

Another black horse, another big stride for horse books! But this black horse is nothing like patient, long-suffering Black Beauty. The Black is a wild stallion who fights anybody unwise enough to approach him. But when he's marooned on an island after a shipwreck, he forms a deep bond with his fellow survivor, a young boy named Alec. This book started a series that continued the Black's adventures and introduced other horses, too.

Easy to find? Yes, in both bookstores and libraries.

Beyond Rope and Fence by David Grew (1922) ^^

This book is like *Black Beauty* gone wild! It stars Queen, a buckskin mare who lives on the prairies of western Canada. Her early experiences with humans aren't good, and her life is a quest for freedom ever after. The author gets into the mind of a horse to tell this tale.

Easy to find? Sort of—you can buy it online. Your library may have it or be able to get it through interlibrary loan.

Jill's Gymkhana by Ruby Ferguson (1949) ^^~
Jill falls in love with a pony in a neighboring farmer's field. The pony soon becomes hers, and this story tells about how she struggles to learn how to ride and care for it. It's the first in a nine-book series. Jill is a very funny, down-to-earth character who gets into some crazy predicaments.
Easy to find? For many years, no! The Jill books were published in Great Britain, so they were hard to find in the United States and Canada. But they're being printed again, and you can find the first few books in the series on Amazon and other bookselling sites. They're just such great books, even if they're not easy to track down.

Last Hurdle by Frieda Kenyon Brown (1953) ^^~
Kathy longs for a horse. One day she buys a neglected gelding from a local farmer, totally surprising her parents! She and her younger brother work hard to care for the horse, Black Baldwin, and to get him fit and ready for riding and showing. Kathy is a realistic character—and Baldy is very "real," too: He's an honest-to-goodness, genuine horse, much like your friendly neighborhood riding-school horse.
Easy to find? Not too hard. This book is out of print, which means you won't find it in bookstores, but you can find used copies online. Many libraries have copies, too.

King of the Wind by Marguerite Henry (1948) ^^~
This book tells the story of the Godolphin Arabian, a horse born in 1724. He's one of the three "founding sires" of the Thoroughbred breed—all Thoroughbreds alive today descend from them. The horse is called Sham, and he's paired up with a stable boy named Agba, who sticks by his side through thick and thin. Marguerite Henry wrote *Misty of Chincoteague* and other classic horse books, too.
Easy to find? Yes, in both bookstores and libraries.

> **Marguerite Henry** once wrote that she was a "boxed-in city mouse as a child." When she grew up, she bought a Morgan gelding named Friday. Friday shared his home with the pony Misty (of *Misty of Chincoteague* fame), a donkey named Brighty, and many cats and dogs.

My Friend Flicka by Mary O'Hara (1941) ^^~
Ken is a quiet, sensitive boy who's cowed by his successful older brother and his well-meaning but short-tempered dad. When Ken gets the chance to pick out a filly or colt of his own, he enrages his dad by choosing Flicka, daughter of the "loco" mare Rocket. As Ken struggles to gain Flicka's trust, he also strives to earn his dad's respect.
Easy to find? Yes, in both bookstores and libraries. Look also for two other books that continue the story: *Thunderhead* and *Green Grass of Wyoming*.

> **Mary O'Hara** didn't grow up with horses, but she was surrounded by them when she moved to a Wyoming ranch after she got married. Some of the scenes in *My Friend Flicka* are based on a real filly that lived on the ranch.

(continued)

National Velvet by Enid Bagnold (1935) ^^~

The classic story of Velvet, a sickly but plucky girl, and the love of her life, The Pie—a headstrong piebald she wins in a raffle. Velvet dreams of entering Pie in a big race called the Grand National, then trains him. All the horses in the story have distinct personalities, and so do Velvet and her three sisters. Girls don't come any horse crazier than Velvet!
Easy to find? Yes, in both bookstores and libraries.

When she was a young girl, **Enid Bagnold** galloped with a paper horse in one hand and a twig for a whip in the other, pretending she was a horse. She also wove ribbons through her toes and pretended to "drive" a team of horses—just like the girl in her book *National Velvet*.

Smoky the Cowhorse by Will James (1926) ^

Smoky's carefree days running wild on the range come to an end when he's roped and tamed by a cowboy, but he quickly finds his new life to be a fun, fascinating challenge. He likes rounding up cows, and he grows deeply fond of the cowboy, who loves him right back. But Smoky's life takes a turn for the worse when a rustler steals him and his band off the winter range. James was a real cowboy who knew how to get into the mind of a horse and tell its story with great feeling.
Easy to find? Yes, in both bookstores and libraries.

Summer Pony by Jean Slaughter Doty (1973) ^^~

Like any horse-crazy girl, Ginny daydreams about having a pony. Then her parents lease a pony for the summer—and she's more of a "nightmare" than a dream horse! Jean Slaughter Doty wrote other fine books about horses, too, such as *If Wishes Were Horses* and *The Winter Pony*.
Easy to find? Yes, in both bookstores and libraries.

Sisters act

Once upon a time there were three horse-crazy English girls, Josephine, Diana, and Christine Pullein-Thompson. They teamed up to write a pony book called *It Began with Picotee*, which was published in 1946. (That year, they were also banned from talking about horses at dinner because they chatted about them so much!) The girls went on to write many more pony books. (Christine wrote more than one hundred!) Their books are very popular in the U.K., and you can find some in Canada and the United States, too.

Sophie Says: Black Beauty: A completely beautiful story of a wonderful, patient horse. **Beyond Rope and Fence:** An amazingly realistic tale of wild mustangs roaming the plains. **Jill's Gymkhana:** A totally fantastic series about a pony-crazy girl and her riding career, starting with her very first pony! **Last Hurdle:** A really realistic story of a horse girl and her own horse.

Top Ten Horse Book Series

The Black Stallion series got its start in 1941 with *The Black Stallion* by Walter Farley. Many, many books later, the series continues with stories written by his son, Steven Farley.

The Breyer Horse Collection series focuses on different horse breeds. Each novel features a horse of a particular breed and tells the story of its life. *Wild Blue*, *Little Prince*, and *Samirah's Ride*, all by Annie Wedekind, are the first three titles in this series.

The Chestnut Hill series by Lauren Brooke is about the adventures of girls staying at a boarding school where riding horses is part of the school day.

The Half Moon Ranch series by Jenny Oldfield focuses on a girl named Kirstie Scott and her horse-filled adventures in the mountains of the Meltwater Range.

The Heartland series by Lauren Brooke is set on a horse farm devoted to helping horses who've been abused or neglected. A girl named Amy works to heal these horses and find them new homes. The series inspired a Canadian TV show by the same name.

The Phantom Stallion series by Terri Farley follows the adventures of a silver stallion and a girl named Samantha. You can find out more online at **www.phantomstallion.com**.

The Pony Club Secrets series by Stacy Gregg stars a girl named Issie, a pony named Blaze, and their friends, both human and equine, at a riding stable. Read about the author and her horses online at **www.stacygregg.co.uk/about.html**.

The Saddle Club series by Bonnie Bryant includes more than a hundred books that tell about the adventures of three girls—Carole, Stevie, and Lisa—and their horses at a stable called Pine Hollow.

The Sandy Lane Stables series by Michelle Bates and Susannah Leigh unfolds at a British riding stable. Each book stars a different horse and rider.

The Thoroughbred series by Joanna Campbell includes more than seventy books about horse racing, eventing, and steeplechasing in Kentucky.

Some All-Around Great Stand-Alone Horse Stories

War Horse by Michael Morpurgo ^^~
Joey, a bay horse beloved by his young owner, leaves his peaceful farm in the English countryside when he is taken by the army to work as a cavalry horse in World War I. The story tells of his adventures as well as the sadness and horror of war, and the horse's hope of meeting his original owner again.

Paint the Wind by Pam Muñoz Ryan ^^~
After the death of her grandmother, young Maya is sent to live on a ranch in Wyoming, where her life story intertwines with a mustang mare named Artemisia.

Chancey of the Maury River by Gigi Amateau ^^~
Chancey is an undervalued, neglected horse who finds reason to hope when he's taken in at a new stable, where he meets a girl named Claire. Claire has also experienced grief and finds healing in teaming up with Chancey.

Top-Ten Nonfiction Horse Books

Horses are endlessly fascinating, so it's no surprise that there are a number of fascinating books about them! Many cover lots of subjects, such as breeds, riding, and horse care. Others focus on one topic, such as stable management or dressage.

This A-to-Z list includes our top-ten nonfiction books—and it was very, very hard to narrow our picks down to ten!

Complete Horse Care Manual by Colin Vogel
First Riding Lessons by Sandy Ransford
Girls and Their Horses (American Girl Library)
Happy Horsemanship by Dorothy Henderson Pinch
How to Think Like a Horse by Cherry Hill
Horse & Pony Care by Sandy Ransford
The New Encyclopedia of the Horse by Elwyn Hartley Edwards
The Ultimate Horse Book by Elwyn Hartley Edwards
The Usborne Complete Book of Riding & Pony Care by Rosie Dickins
   and Gill Harvey
A Young Rider's Guide: Learn to Ride by Carolyn Henderson

Horse Magazines

There are horse magazines geared for every type of rider, horse enthusiast, and breeder. Many are written for professionals, but others can be enjoyed by any fan.

Some general magazines include *Horse Illustrated, Horse & Rider, The Canadian Horse Journal,* and *Equus.* There are also fabulous horse magazines written especially for horse-crazy girls like you!

Blaze calls itself the "magazine for horse-crazy kids." It's packed with info, stories, jokes, and pictures of horses, and also offers lots of contests with great prizes. The magazine's website is **www.blazekids.com**. (See also page 111.)

Horsepower is a magazine aimed at horse-crazy kids across North America. Find out more about it on the website of the magazine *Horse-Canada*: **www.horse-canada.com/horsepower/about.shtml**. (See also page 112.)

Young Rider magazine is filled with stories about horses, riders, horse rescuers, and other horse people. You'll find pictures galore and posters, too, as well as how-to articles. The magazine's website is **www.youngrider.com**. (See also page 113.)

Sophie Says:
Blaze: The best horse/pony magazine ever!

"Just About Horses" Magazine

Model horse collectors and customizers turn to *Just About Horses* for info and advice about their hobby. It has articles about Breyer models, tips on repainting and remaking horses, and suggestions for setting up scenes for photo and live shows. For short, the magazine is called *JAH!* www.breyerhorses.com/jah/

Got a Kid Sister?

Maybe you have a horse-crazy little sister . . . or cousin. Maybe you babysit some horse-crazy little girls. Why not share some of the horse books you liked when you were little—or newer books that you know you'd have loved at their age? Here are some they might enjoy:

Charming Ponies series by Lois K. Szymanski

Horse and Pony Treasury by Rosie Dickens and Leonie Pratt

Keeker and the Sneaky Pony series by Hadley Higginson

My First Horse and Pony Book by Judith Draper and Matthew Roberts

My Magical Pony series by Jenny Oldfield

My Secret Unicorn series by Linda Chapman

Pony-Crazed Princess series by Diana Kimpton

Pony Pals series by Jeanne Betancourt

Wind Dancers series by Sibley Miller

Magic, Mythical Horses

Have you ever cuddled up with a stuffed unicorn? Magical horses leaped out of the human imagination long, long ago. They appear in ancient stories, or "myths," along with other breeds of steeds you'll never see at a local stable. Here are a few:

Riding on the Wind

Pegasus, the flying horse, is the most famous mythological steed. He has a strange pedigree. His father was Poseidon, god of the sea and of horses. His mother was Medusa, a monster with poisonous snakes for hair who could turn you to stone with just one look. His foaling was even weirder: He popped up when an ancient Greek hero lopped off his monstrous mother's head.

Horse with a Horn

The **unicorn** is a white horse that sports a long, spiral horn on his forehead. He often has deerlike legs and a beard, like a goat. The horn was believed to be able to cure a person unlucky enough to drink poison. The unicorn himself could clean up dirty water just by touching it with his horn.

    A unicorn is said to be fierce and fast. A unicorn would only allow itself to be caught by a young, sweet girl. When he saw such a girl, he would gallop to her, settle down beside her, lay his head in her lap, and fall asleep!

Almost Human

A **centaur** is a creature that is half human, half horse. Centaurs appear in ancient Greek stories as a bunch of fierce, badly behaved party animals. One centaur, however, was famous for teaching a hero of ancient Greece how to ride. He also taught a Greek god how to heal people's injuries. More recently, centaurs have been spotted on the grounds of a school for witches and wizards in J. K. Rowling's Harry Potter books!

Horses on the Web

What does "www" stand for? "Whinny, whinny, whinny," of course. You can use horsey websites to learn about horses, chat about horses with other horse girls, and play horse games. There's even a show just for horse girls called Horsegirltv.com! (More on that below.)

Informational Sites

There are many, many websites about horses. The ones listed here are ones we've checked out and think you'll enjoy.

Caution! An Internet search can turn up lots of websites that aren't what you're looking for! *Make sure your parents or another trusted adult know you're using the Internet when you do a search.* You may also have better luck finding the right sites if you search on a school computer.

All Horses

www.allhorses.info
All horses, all the time! Loads of articles and pictures here.

American Horse Council

www.horsecouncil.org
The American Horse Council is an association that works with the U.S. government on issues related to horses. It's a useful site to visit if you want to find out about laws and regulations regarding horses. The issues range from making racing safer for racehorses to making sure public lands are kept open for use by riders.

American Museum of Natural History

www.amnh.org/exhibitions/horse
This museum in New York City has the world's largest collection of horse fossils. It recently had an exhibit all about horses, and put lots of great info about them on this site.

Blaze

www.blazekids.com
The website of *Blaze*, a magazine for horse-loving kids, has lots of info, as well as puzzles and contests.

Dream Horse

www.dreamhorse.com

This site lists horses for sale in the United States. You can search this site and dream about horses you'd buy if you could—and fuel your dreams for the future.

eXtension Initiative

www.horsequest.com

This site offers videos and info about horses and stable management. Horse experts from universities answer submitted questions.

GirlsHorseClub

www.girlshorseclub.com

Horsey blogs, book reviews, links to games, contests, online art gallery, and more.

Horse-Canada

www.horse-canada.com

This site is the "Horse Source" for Canada and has news and links about equestrian events across North America.

Horsecrazygirls.com

www.horsecrazygirls.com

This site was created by a mom and her horse-crazy daughter. It's a round-up of horsey places you can visit on the Web, such as game sites, free-art sites, videos, and the like. You can join a free club and write online reviews of games and other products.

Horsefun

http://horsefun.com

Horsefun offers info about horses as well as games, puzzles, riding tips, and stories for horse lovers.

Horsegirl TV

www.horsegirltv.com

A world of horse info awaits you here. This site offers dozens of videos about all aspects of horsemanship and horse care, as well as podcasts. It's hosted by a woman named Angelea Kelly Walkup, who's ridden all her life and won prizes in dressage.

Horse Channel

www.horsechannel.com

This site has tons of info about horse breeds and other equine topics.

International Horse Club

www.internationalhorseclub.com
Fun facts, how-to and training videos, quizzes, contests, and games.

Junior Master Horseman

www.juniormasterhorseman.com
This site is a co-production of the American Youth Horse Council and the American Quarter Horse Association. You can sign up for an interactive program and buy a book that will help you study to be a Junior Master Horseman—even if you don't have a horse (yet!).

Kentucky Horse Park "Just for Kids"

www.kyhorsepark.com/kids
The Kentucky Horse Park in Lexington, Kentucky, is horse-girl heaven. This site has tons of info about horses.

Oklahoma State University "Horse Breeds"

www.ansi.okstate.edu/breeds/horses
You'll find an A-Z listing of horse breeds, with info on each one, here.

Pony Club

www.ponyclub.org (in USA)
www.canadianponyclub.org (in Canada)
A Pony Club website is useful for you if you own a pony or have the use of one. Pony Clubs offer programs and events for young riders.

Pony Magazine

www.ponymag.com
There's lots of horsey stuff to enjoy on this website for *Pony*, a British magazine for kids who are "horse mad," as they say across the Atlantic!

Young Rider

www.youngrider.com
Young Rider, a horse magazine for kids, offers lots of things for horse lovers on their website.

> **Sophie Says: Young Rider** is packed with info about owning a horse! They have really good posters, too!

Unwanted Horse Coalition

www.unwantedhorsecoalition.org
Sadly, horses can be unwanted and even abandoned. This organization educates people about responsible horse ownership. It also helps owners who can't keep their horses and sets guidelines for horse-rescue groups.

Online Horse Games

Hop around on the Internet and you'll find lots of jumping, racing, and other games with horses. Some cost money. Others are free to join but cost for upgrades. A few are totally free. Here are a few sites that are very popular with horse-crazy girls.

Bella Sara

www.bellasara.com

Train, care for, and play with magical horses, or enjoy puzzles and games. First you'll need to get Bella Sara cards in order to play online.

Club Pony Pals

www.clubponypals.com

You can choose a pony, groom it, and ride it on this free website. It's based on the popular Pony Pals book series by Jeanne Betancourt.

Horse Isle

www.horseisle.com

Catch a wild horse and go on adventures in this multi-player game. Collect gems and other treasures as you carry out quests. Care for and train your horse, then compete against other players.

Horseland

www.horseland.com

Ride horses, explore and create horse shows, and compete with other players in this online world. You can also design your own "avatar"— an on-screen character who represents you.

Howrse

www.howrse.com

Breed, raise, and train horses as you manage your own equestrian center.

My Stable

www.mystable.co.uk

Breed, train, care for, and show horses on this British website.

Online Horse Games

www.naturalhorsetraining.com/OnlineGames2.html

This isn't a game itself, but it has tons of links to horse games!

Ponybox

www.ponybox.com

Buy, sell, train, and compete your ponies here.

Pony Island

www.ponyisland.net

Breed, raise, train, and play with magical multi-colored ponies.

More Horse Games (No electricity needed!)

You can play horse games even without the help of batteries and electrical outlets. Here are some favorite non-electronic horse games.

Herd Your Horses! (TaliCor)

In this board game, players can be mustang stallions vying to round up mares and keep their herds together as they journey to a hidden pasture. They can also take the roles of ranchers rounding up horses. Each horse card features an individual equine with its own name, breed, and history. You can also play the game alone if none of your friends can come over. And, you can use the cards separately from the game in role-playing games, too.

Horse-Opoly (Vintage Sports Cards, Inc.)

Like Monopoly? Like horses? Then Monopoly + horses = the game for you! Each set of properties on the board is devoted to a breed of horse. Playing pieces include things like a boot and a horsefly. Instead of hotels and houses, you buy barns and hay bales.

Horse Lover's Monopoly (USAopoly)

Horse-trading, Monopoly style! Build up stables of your favorite breeds in this version of the popular game. The board features photos of horses, and playing pieces include a little horse.

Horse Show (Gamewright)

In this card game, players figure out which of their stable of horses is the best choice to compete in the event that turns up on a drawn card—either a show-jumping, hunter, dressage, or equitation event. The more events you win, the more blue-ribbon cards you gather.

Sophie Says: Horse Isle: I am entirely addicted to this game. I make online friends and catch horses. They have more than eighty-eight breeds. What's not to like? **Howrse:** A really great game! **My Stable:** You can catch wild horses and make your own pictures for them. **Herd Your Horses!:** The greatest horse board game I know! **Horse Show:** The best horse card game I've ever played!

Top Ten Horse Computer Games

There are lots of horse games for home computers and handheld game devices that give you a chance to groom, tack up, ride, and train virtual horses of your own. Here are ten that wound up in our winner's circle.

The Equestrian
(IGS; Windows Vista, XP, Me, 2000, '98)

Train your horse and compete in jumping, cross-country, and dressage. Your skills expand as you work with your horse, which has its own unique temperament and skill set that must be taken into account as you train. This game has a stamp of approval from the USEF (United States Equestrian Federation).

Gallop and Ride
(THQ; Nintendo Wii)

Create your dream horse, then care for it and train it. Go riding on a beach or take a trek through mountains. You can also fix up your ranch and add new buildings to it.

Let's Ride: Friends Forever
(THQ; Windows Vista, XP, Me; Nintendo DS)

Be best friends with your very own horse—a horse you can put together yourself from a wide variety of breeds, manes, tails, and tack tidbits. Enter competitions and keep a journal of your accomplishments.

Let's Ride: Riding Star
(ValuSoft; Windows Vista, XP)

Reward your hardworking horse with new saddles and blankets as you win ribbons in cross-country, show-jumping, and dressage events. New courses and prizes await you as you tackle competitions. You can also just care for your horse and go for a hack.

Let's Ride: Silver Buckle Stables
(THQ; Windows XP; Playstation 2)

Customize your first horse, give it a name, then gallop off on trails and do some barrel racing. You can change your horse's color and name whenever you want, and you can unlock a few more horses as you play. (You can also race around barrels in Let's Ride: Corral Club.)

Lucinda Green's Equestrian Challenge
(Red Mile; Windows XP, Me, '98; Playstation 2)

Choose the breed and color of your horse, give it a name, then care for it and train it before competing in cross-country, show-jumping, and dressage events. This game challenges you with a variety of jumping courses, and you can unlock new horses and equipment as you play. You'll get advice from Lucinda Green, a British Olympic rider.

My Horse and Me
(Atari; Windows XP; Nintendo Wii, Nintendo DS)

Choose your horse's color, feed and groom your horse, then train with a personal coach before competing on show-jumping courses worldwide. You can also play some fun mini-games. The FEI (Fédération Equestre Internationale), an organization dedicated to Olympic horse sports, gave its seal of approval to this game.

Petz Horsez 2
(UBI Soft; Nintendo Wii, DS; Playstation 2; Windows Vista, XP)

Follow the growth of your foals as you raise and train them from birth. Enter competitions, spiff up your horses, and enjoy the plot twists and turns in a choose-your-own-adventure story as you go along.

Riding Star
(Valcon Games; Playstation 2)

Customize, care for, and train horses, then compete in dressage, show-jumping, and cross-country events. You can ride your horse in a world-famous arena in Germany or just take it out for a leisurely ride in the countryside. Each horse has its own personality and quirks.

Saddle Up with Pippa Funnell
(UBI Soft; Windows XP)

Solve a mystery as you fix up an old horse farm, train a stable full of horses, and strive to become a top equestrian in three-day eventing competitions. Breeds of horses you can own include Andalusians and Lipizzans. As you play, you'll get advice from Pippa Funnell, a champion British rider who competes in three-day eventing.

Sophie Says: Let's Ride: Silver Buckle Stables: I like that you can create your own horse, win more horses, and unlock new items. **Lucinda Green's Equestrian Challenge:** A really realistic game! Challenging jumping, dressage, and cross-country. Excellent scenery!

The World of Model Horses

Do you have statues of horses cantering along shelves and bookcases in your room? For horseless horse girls, model horses are the next best thing. Not only can you play with and admire your models, you can make tack and build stables for them.

You can also kick the hobby up a bit and immerse yourself in the world of model horse showing.

Model Horse Shows

Showing a model horse involves creating everything from realistic tack to a miniature world to surround it. You also have a choice of classes in which to show your model horses.

A halter class is one example. The models are most often shown based on breeds. Judges study each model's body shape, or "conformation." They judge how well each model's conformation and color meets the standard for its breed, just as if it were a real horse. A rare model might attract a judge's eye, just as a special horse might in real life. But scratches and other marks on a model may knock off points.

In a performance class, a model horse is placed in a setting. You can think of it as a moment frozen in time, just like a photo of a real horse in a competition. The setting is made to look as realistic as possible, with everything in the scene being the right size in relation to the horse. The horse itself is posed in different ways depending on the class. It may simply be standing, or it may be caught in mid-stride as it races around a barrel.

Every little detail counts in setting up a scene for a performance class! For starters, you need to know what tack a horse is required to wear and how it should fit. A horse in a Western performance class, for example, might need two cinches, a breastplate, or a saddle with a specially shaped

A Model Is Born

A model horse starts out as a clay figure. This clay horse is sculpted by an artist who's studied how horses are shaped and how they move. (It's a pretty cool career for a horse lover who's also got a flair for art!) When the clay horse looks just right, it's used to make a metal mold—basically, a hollow metal horse.

Next, hot, liquid plastic is put inside the mold. It cools in the shape of a horse. Then it's removed so that artists can paint it.

skirt. You also must know how a horse moves and where it would be in relation to a barrel, a jump, or other feature. A show hunter, for example, must be placed the right distance from the jump it's about to leap over. (Plus the jump must be the right kind for the event, or you'll lose points!)

Performance classes include many of the same ones you'd see at a real horse show: dressage, show jumping, and reining. There are also classes for Arabian costume—a favorite for collectors who like to research and make tack! A show may even have classes for "fantasy" horses, such as unicorns.

At a "live show," competitors set up their horses on tables that function as show rings. But you can show your horses even if you can't travel to a live show. You can enter them in "photo shows." These shows have classes just like live shows. To enter, you photograph your models and send the images to the judges.

Want to learn more about model horse shows? Hop online and visit these sites:

Model Horse Guide This collectors' site provides loads of info about the model horse hobby. You'll find links to articles about photo and live shows: www.modelhorseguide.com/breyerhowtos.htm.

North American Model Horse Shows Association

This association is the leading organization for the model horse world in the United States and Canada, and oversees many shows. You'll know a show comes under NAMHSA's umbrella if it's listed as being NAMHSA approved.

Every year, NAMHSA holds a big North American championship model horse show. In even-numbered years, the show is held in Lexington, Kentucky. In odd-numbered years, it's held elsewhere—check the NAMHSA website to find out where. Find out more at www.namhsa.org.

BreyerFest®

Every July, the Kentucky Horse Park in Lexington, Kentucky, is home to Breyer-Fest—a lollapalooza of a model horse festival sponsored by model horse maker Breyer. Thousands of collectors from all over the United States and Europe flock to this festival to swap and show their models. You can come to compete, or just to mix and mingle with people who like model horses as much as you do.

To find out more about BreyerFest, go to **www.breyerhorses.com/breyerfest**. To read about making setups and other topics, look for articles at **www.breyerhorses.com**.

Breyer Animal Creations®

Ask any horse girl to name just one company that makes model horses, and chances are she'll respond, "Breyer."

Breyer got its start as a plastic molding company. In 1950, it produced its first model horse. This steed, known as the Western Horse, was created to stand on a base along with a clock. To Breyer's surprise, people began clamoring to buy just the horse. The company made this wish come true and then began molding other kinds of horses.

Today, Breyer's stable includes dozens of horse breeds in a rainbow of colors. Horses range in size from tiny Mini Whinnies that can perch on your finger to the big "Traditional"-size models (which are about one-ninth the size of a real horse—the technical way to say this is that they're in 1:9 scale). Every year, about five million horses gallop out of Breyer's production lines and onto the shelves of stores.

Find out more about Breyer Animal Creations at **www.breyerhorses.com**.

Make a Scene!

For starters, if you're showing a horse in a performance class that requires tack, you've got to make sure it's wearing the right stuff! A rule book will list exactly what your horse needs to wear in a class.

You'll also be setting the stage for your horse. Are you entering him in a barrel-racing event? Then you'll need a sandy surface, a rider, and barrels. Is he approaching a jump in a hunter competition? Then you'll need to set up a realistic jump and supply a rider, too.

You can buy many of the props, but many model horse fans find that much of the fun lies in making their own props or finding bits and pieces to turn into mini versions of barrels, jumps, and even hoof picks and buckets!

Get inspired by looking at books and magazines written for hobbyists who set up dollhouses or model railroads. These sources have great ideas for turning everyday items into mini horse gear. You can also find tips on model horse websites.

Model Makeovers

Most horse girls take care not to drop their model horses or let them get nicked or scratched. So what inspires some to dunk their models in scalding-hot water or even cut off their heads?

What these collectors are doing is called "customizing." Customizing a model means repainting it or repositioning its body parts—or both.

Hot water softens a plastic model so its body parts can be gently moved. Cutting off parts of the horse is necessary if a model's position is going to be drastically changed—for example, if a standing horse is being turned into a galloping one.

A collector may customize a model horse to perfect its conformation and make it look even more like the breed it represents. A model may be remade to change its gait or even to change its breed. Some collectors also like to replace a horse's plastic mane and tail with silky fibers such as mohair, which is very realistic. Or a model may simply be repainted to give it a preferred color or markings such as spots, socks, or a star.

Customized horses can be shown in both halter and performance classes. Halter classes are designed to feature either original horses (horses that haven't been customized) or customized ones.

If you're interested in customizing, you can find info online at *Model Horse Guide*: www.modelhorseguide.com/breyerhowtos.htm.

This collectors' site is chock-full of info about model horses. It provides links to how-to articles about repainting horses, adding mohair manes and tails, and the like.

How Collectible
Is Your Model Horse?

It's easy to know what Breyer horse you're getting when you buy or receive one that's new in the box. But what about older ones that turn up at flea markets, on auction websites, and the like? Just who are these mysterious horses? Breyer has made models for more than sixty years, after all—and some of the oldest are quite valuable.

Wonder no more. There are many ways to find out more about your model. For starters, look for these collectors' guides at your library or local bookstore (or online):

•*Breyer Animal Collector's Guide* by Felicia Browell (online at **www.collectorbooks.com**)

•*Breyer Molds & Models* by Nancy Atkinson Young (online at **www.schifferbooks.com**)

Sophie Says: My favorite toy horses are Breyer horses. I collect the "classics" size. They are so amazingly life-like! On my last sleepover, my friend and I stayed up until 3 a.m. playing a game with them. They are the best models ever! Every horse girl, check them out!

Pony Party

Horses are not only a great dream for your life, they're a great theme for your party! You can have a horsey birthday party even if you can't have a horse or pony actually attend it (though you may be able to find a traveling pony party or a local stable that hosts birthdays).

Try brainstorming ideas for a pony party with your friends. Here are a few fun ideas and activities to get you started.

Decorations

Set the stage for your party with horsey decor!

 • Have a Western party—draw or paint cactuses on large sheets of paper and cut them out to hang on walls and doors; give out bandannas for your guests to wear.

 • Draw horses on large sheets of paper and hang them on doors and walls.

 • Put your stuffed horses and your old rocking horse or stick horse to good use as decorations.

Food

At your pony party, you could serve:

 • sliced apples, baby carrots, and oatmeal cookies for a snack

 • oatmeal for breakfast, if it's a sleepover

 • a carrot cake as your birthday cake—or at least a horse-shaped cake!

 • hay-and-horse treats (spaghetti and meatballs) for dinner, or chuck-wagon chow such as franks and beans for a Western-theme party

Games and Activities

 • Write assorted horse behaviors and gaits on slips of paper, such as "Neigh," "Trot," and "Roll Over." (If your friends are ultra-horsey, you can try fancier horse terms, such as "Piaffe" and "Capriole"!) Each player draws a slip and then carries out the action named on it.

 • Play a horse-themed game of charades.

 • Paint each other's faces with pictures of horses; you can also paint your faces to look like horses.

 • Make popcorn and watch a horse movie suggested in this book.

 • Go outside and play horseshoes.

 • Paint model horses in kits that come with paints and brushes.

Pipe-cleaner Pony

All you need to make a stable's worth of ponies is a pack of pipe cleaners. (Colorful, thicker ones you buy in craft stores are great, too. They're called chenille sticks.)

You'll need at least four pipe cleaners to make a basic horse.

1. Place one pipe cleaner on a tabletop. This will form the head, neck, and body.
2. Make an X with two of the other pipe cleaners and put them on top of the first. Don't put the cross of the X right in the middle—keep it more to one end, about a third of the way up the pipe cleaner's length. They will soon be your horse's legs.
3. Pinch the place where all three pipe cleaners meet to hold them together. Bend all four of the legs down.
4. Bring each leg up again so that it goes under the body and up the other side.
5. Then bend each leg again so that it wraps back across the top and down over the other side. This will affix the legs firmly to the body. Figure out how long you want the pipe-cleaner legs to be, then cut them. (Fold up the tip of each leg to hide the sharp end of the wire.)
6. The longer end of the "body" pipe cleaner becomes the head and neck. Form a head by making a loop at the top and wrapping the tip around the top of the neck.
7. See the short pipe-cleaner bit that's still sticking out of the tail end? Fold it and wrap it around the body to fatten it. Then take the fourth pipe cleaner and wrap it around and around the head, neck, and body to flesh out the horse. Use more pipe cleaners if you have them to continue adding bulk.
8. Now you can glue on details, such as a yarn mane and tail, felt ears and eyes, and the like. You can glue on felt saddles and blankets, too. This horse can be posed in many positions. Try making a little rider for him, too!

Party Favors

- Little plastic horses, small wind-up toy horses, or tiny flocked horses
- Pens or pencils with horses on them
- Tiny notepads with horses on the cover
- Peppermints (horses love 'em!)
- Horsey bracelets, rings, necklaces, or charms
- Miniature horse-themed coloring books
- Jelly beans—Pack them in snack-size zip-locking bags, then add labels with made-up horsey flavor names (e.g., Blue Roan, Green Grass, Purple Palomino, Chocolate Taffy)
- Cards with horses on them, such as Bella Sara cards

Equine Art and Artists

Do you doodle horses in the margins of your notebooks? If so, this section's especially for you!

A Lightning-Fast Top Ten Tour of Horse-Art History

Don't blink, because this tour is quick as a wink! People have been painting ponies and sculpting steeds for thousands of years, so we'll just gallop through this gallery-in-time and narrow it down to our Top Ten.

3,300 years ago in ancient Egypt: Horses leap like gazelles across vases, urns, and the walls of tombs. Many of them are warhorses. They wear fancy trappings and pull chariots. Horses in the same scene are usually all mirror images of each other.

31,000 years ago in Europe: Prehistoric people paint horses on the walls of caves in Europe. They look a lot like Przewalski's horses. (See page 68.) Chunky horses like this continue to be painted on caves for the next 25,000 years. Prehistoric people also carve tiny horses out of mammoth ivory, antlers, bones, and stones. Some are even worn as pendants—just like you might do today.

2,500 years ago in ancient Rome: Chariot horses prance across murals made of tiles. Ancient Romans gaze in awe at four gigantic, real-looking bronze horses in one of their cities. If you visit Venice, Italy, today, you can still see the Four Horses of St. Mark's in a museum.

2,000 years ago in China: An unknown artist creates a beautiful little bronze horse pacing with its head and tail up. It balances on one foot atop a little bronze bird called a swallow, which is a symbol of speed. Archaeologists dig up the statue in 1969, and it becomes world famous.

176: You read that right—the Equestrian Statue of Marcus Aurelius really was made so long ago that the year has only three numerals! This statue shows a powerful warhorse carrying an emperor of Rome. It's copied many times by other sculptors and inspires others across the centuries. You can see the original in the Capitoline Museum in Rome, Italy.

1603: European artist Peter Paul Rubens paints a portrait of a nobleman riding a stunning white horse. The beautiful steed has kind, liquid eyes and a rippling mane. It's just one of many, many stunning horses that appear in portraits of royalty at this time.

1762: British artist George Stubbs paints a gigantic portrait of a racehorse named Whistlejacket. The picture is nearly 10 feet tall (3 m) and about 8 feet (2.4 m) wide, so the horse is life-size. He appears on a plain background, without any tack or rider on him. Stubbs writes and illustrates a book on horse anatomy a few years later. He also paints many other horses' portraits. You can see *Whistlejacket* at the National Gallery in London.

1853: French artist Rosa Bonheur, who studied horses carefully and sketched them constantly, paints a gigantic work of art called *The Horse Fair*. It's about 8 feet (2.4 m) tall and half as long as a school bus. You can see it today at The Metropolitan Museum of Art in New York City.

1898: American artist Frederic Remington sculpts a bucking bronco dumping a cowboy on the ground. He calls the bronze statue *The Wicked Pony*. It's just one of many horses he sculpts, draws, and paints in his lifetime. His work is like a history book of the Old West.

1998: The face of Native American leader Crazy Horse peers from the side of a mountain near Custer, South Dakota. Now his stallion is slowly being carved. This horse will be so big when he's done, you could fit a five-room house in each of his nostrils! The sculpture got its start in 1948 and nobody knows exactly when it will be finished.

Crazy about Horse Art?

Horses pop up a lot in art through the ages. They appear on everything from ancient cups and bowls to wall-size tapestries. Many artists still make horses the focus of their work today. If you'd like to explore equine art, you can get started with these books and websites:

The Horse: 30,000 Years of the Horse in Art by Tamsin Pickeral is a huge, beautiful book packed with pictures of horse art from prehistoric times right up to 2006, when it was published.

Another good book to track down is *The Horse in Art* by John Baskett, also published in 2006.

There's also a magazine all about horse art, called *Art Horse Magazine*. Look for it online at **www.arthorsemagazine.com**.

Penning Ponies

Horses are often said to be one of the most difficult animals to draw—so if you doodle them, doodle lots. (Just not in class!) Sketch from real life if you can. Study photographs from newspapers and nonfiction books. You'll also find some great illustrations of horses in children's books.

Here are a few artists you might like:

Margot Apple (a great name for a horse artist!) keeps three horses at home. The rest of her ponies canter through books such as *Runaway Radish* and *Birthday Pony*.

Kenneth Lilly draws many kinds of animals. You can find his horses in the picture book *A Field Full of Horses*.

C. W. Anderson rode, wrote about, and drew horses. He's most famous for his stories about a boy named Billy and his pony, Blaze.

Sam Savitt wanted to be a horse when he grew up. That proved impossible, so he became a horseman and horse illustrator instead! You can find his work in books for horse-crazy people of any age. Check online at **www.samsavitt.com**.

Wesley Dennis illustrated many of Marguerite Henry's horse stories. Check out his work in the book *Album of Horses*.

Jared D. Lee is an artist who has illustrated many children's books. Among horse people, he's best known for his funny cartoons about horses. Find the books *Talk to the Hoof* and *I'm at the End of My Rope and You're Tugging at It*, and start laughing out loud!

Short and Stout

Have you ever ridden on a "Thelwell pony"? No, this isn't a little-known breed! A Thelwell pony is a short, fat, fuzzy, bad-tempered pony drawn by British cartoonist Norman Thelwell.

Thelwell lived from 1923 to 2004. He drew hundreds of cartoons about little girls and their chunky, badly behaved ponies. Among his characters were a pony named Kipper and his girl, Penelope. You can see some of his work online at **www.thelwell.org.uk/images/ponies/index.htm**.

How to Draw a Horse

Love to draw horses? You can pick up tips from some excellent horse artists who have written about their craft.

One great source is *Draw Horses with Sam Savitt.* Savitt brought to his work a lifetime of experience with horses. In addition to illustrating books and charts about horses, Savitt also served as the official artist of the U.S. Equestrian Team.

Another book to look for is *Anyone Can Draw Horses!* by horse lover and artist June Evers. Evers provides step-by-step instructions as well as pictures you can trace and decorate. There's something in her book for everyone, from beginners to more experienced artists.

You can also hop online for a drawing lesson. Illustrator Jan Brett has a video called "How to Draw Horses" on her website at www.janbrettvideos.com/how_to_draw_horses_high_bandwidth.htm.

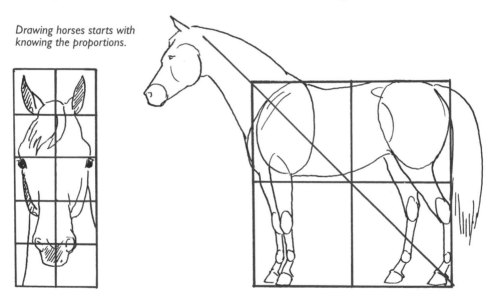

Drawing horses starts with knowing the proportions.

Horses in Chalk

Giant white horses loom on scattered hillsides in England and Scotland. These horses were created by carving the land after clearing it of plants so that the white, chalky rock underneath was revealed. Some of the horses have a known history. Others are more than 300 years old, and their origins are shrouded in mystery.

The most famous chalk steed is the Uffington White Horse, which gallops across a hillside in Oxfordshire in England. It's about 3,000 years old. At 365 feet (111.2 m) long, it's the biggest chalk horse of them all. So far, no one is sure who carved it.

Poetry in Motion

Part of the joy in riding a horse or watching one move is the pleasant rhythm of its motion.

The beauty of a horse's motion is paired up with music to create wonderful shows. A dressage competition, for example, may include a musical ride. Circuses often feature "liberty horses," which move around a ring without riders on their backs. Dancing horses are also at the heart of some famous shows that tour in North America from time to time. Here are a few that may come to a city or fairground near you!

The "World-Famous" Lipizzaner Stallions

The "World-Famous" Lipizzaner stallions perform a dazzling "horse ballet" in arenas across North America every year. The beautiful white horses do dressage and also perform the "airs above the ground"—the prancing, rearing, and leaping that were once used by mounted soldiers on European battlefields long ago. The show also features Andalusians, the spirited horses who were the ancestors of the Lipizzan breed.

You can find out more about this show, as well as see videos of the horses, online at www.lipizzaner.com.

The Spanish Riding School

The Winter Riding Hall in Vienna, Austria, is like a palace for horses: a vast room with tall white columns and arches in the ceiling. It's the home of the famous Spanish Riding School—the oldest riding school in the world. It dates back to 1572 and is named after the Spanish horses used at that time.

PRANCING, DANCING HORSES

If you can't get enough of beautiful horses who move as if they're ballet dancers, here's a troupe you can enjoy: **Zingaro** is a theatre group that includes about thirty horses, as well as riders, dancers, and musicians. The show celebrates the bond between horses and humans, and how it is expressed in different cultures around the world. Visit Zingaro at www.zingaro.fr/.

Riders at the School learn to ride and train beautiful Lipizzan stallions. The riding they do is called "haute école." This means "high school," but not the kind with lockers and lunchrooms, of course! It refers to a type of riding that is like a kind of deluxe dressage. The horses are schooled so that their natural movements are shaped and controlled to bring out their beauty. Stallions that rise to the top of the class learn the "airs above the ground."

Gorgeous Whites

White Stallion of Lipizza by Marguerite Henry is a story about the Spanish Riding School. There is also a gorgeous large-screen movie about Lipizzans called *Majestic White Horses*. It's hard to find, but if you live near an IMAX theater, keep an eye on its listings to see if this movie shows up there.

The School breeds all its own horses. The Lipizzans are born black or bay. Most of them slowly turn white as they grow older, but some bay horses stay bay. The School includes one bay horse in its performances as a tradition—he's a good-luck token.

In 2008, the School broke with one tradition—having all male riders—by admitting two young women for training. (This training can last from ten to fifteen years and includes teaching your horses.) So you can now add "become a rider at the Spanish Riding School" to your career goals!

To find out more about the School, visit its site at www.srs.at. (The text on the site is in German, but you'll find a button you can select to change it to English.)

A Showstopper!

Lorenzo is a rider in France who performs stunts with a dozen horses. He's known as "The Flying Frenchman." See him in action, and you'll see why! In one showstopper, he stands atop two horses as they leap over a series of jumps. He even does this while holding the reins of several other horses who jump along with his mounts!

Cavalia

Cavalia is a celebration of the bond between horses and people. It blends music, dance, and acrobatics with horses in motion. More than thirty horses perform in the show, including quarter horses, Belgian draft horses, and Lusitanos.

Some of Cavalia's acts are beautiful, mysterious dressage performances that look like dreams. Others are exciting, fast-moving performances with trick riders—including Roman riders, who stand on the backs of galloping horses. Sometimes, horses appear on stage without any riders.

To find out more, check out Cavalia's website at www.cavalia.net.

Horses Coast-to-Coast

Going on a vacation in the United States or Canada? If you're lucky, your destination may be a totally horsey place, such as a dude ranch or a national park with a nearby stable that offers trail rides. If so, finding a way to include riding in your trip will be a no-brainer.

Other times, however, you'll have to work harder to shoehorn horses into the trip—and that's where research comes in handy.

Pony Places and Horsey Happenings

Say your family's planning to camp on a beach. Chances are there's a stable in the area where you can rent a horse and ride along the shore. Heading for the hills? Well, mountains and trail rides go together like macaroni and cheese.

How do you find them? Here are two options:

Get a travel guide about the place you're visiting. Then look for "horseback riding" or "stables" in the index.

Go online and search for "riding stables" along with the name of the place where you'll be vacationing. You can make this search general ("riding stables Oregon coast") or specific ("riding stables Florence, Oregon").

You can also look for websites that are all about planning a horse-happy trip. The site Horse and Travel, for example, includes all fifty states and the stables you'll find in them (www.horseandtravel.com).

Even if you can't visit these places in person, visit their websites—they have a lot to offer. Happy trails!

Northeastern United States

Learn about harness racing at the Harness Racing Museum in Goshen, New York. It's right next door to Goshen's racetrack, the oldest harness track in the world! Standardbreds have raced there since 1838. www.harnessmuseum.com

Gallop over to the National Museum of Racing in Saratoga Springs, New York, where you can ride on a mechanical horse in a racing simulator! The museum also has tons of cool racing equipment, such as a starting gate, and a racehorse skeleton to study. www.racingmuseum.org

Saratoga Springs, New York, is also where you'll find Saratoga Race-track, where Thoroughbreds race in August and a few days in July and September. During that short racing season, the track offers "Breakfast at Saratoga" on Saturdays. You can arrive early in the morning, watch horses work out, and even take a tour of the stable area.
www.nyra.com/Saratoga/GeneralInformation/Kids/Kids.shtml

At other times of the year, you can eat breakfast bright and early while watching horses zip by at Belmont Park in Elmont, New York.
www.nyra.com/Belmont/GeneralInformation/Kids/Kids.shtml

Find out a thing or two about Morgans at the National Museum of the Morgan Horse in Shelburne, Vermont. www.morganmuseum.org

You can sometimes visit real Morgans at the University of Vermont Morgan Horse Farm in Burlington, Vermont. There are special "Foal Days" in June and a big open house in August, plus tours are often available, too.
http://asci.uvm.edu/morgan

The United States Equestrian Team Foundation headquarters and training center in Gladstone, New Jersey, is the home of the U.S. team that competes in the Olympics and other world equestrian events. Guided tours are often available. www.uset.com

Southeastern United States

Kentucky! This is a state of pure joy for horse girls—it's horses, horses, horses 24/7. First stop: The Kentucky Horse Park in Lexington (www.kyhorsepark.com). It's a horse paradise featuring about fifty breeds of horses; mares and foals; champion Thoroughbreds; riding; shows; and tours. It's also where you'll find the American Saddlebred Museum (www.americansaddlebredmuseum.org) and the spectacular International Museum of the Horse (www.imh.org). It's also where model horses take center stage every year in mid-July during BreyerFest. That's when collectors from around the world gather to show their model horses. Events featuring live horses are part of the festival, too. Find out more about BreyerFest on page 119, as well as at www.breyerhorses.com/breyerfest.

Kentucky's also famous for the Kentucky Derby, which is run the first Saturday in May at Churchill Downs in Louisville. The track also boasts its own Kentucky Derby Museum: www.derbymuseum.org.

Kentucky is also home to the Rolex Kentucky Three-Day Event, which is held at the Kentucky Horse Park. Horses and riders compete in dressage, cross-country, and arena jumping. This yearly event spans three days that include the last weekend in April. www.rk3de.org/index.php

Wild "Banker Ponies" roam the national seashores of North Carolina's Outer Banks. You can look for them on your own or go on a guided tour. When you're done, learn more about them at the Corolla Wild Horse Fund's museum in Old Corolla Village: www.corollawildhorses.com.

Run, don't walk, to the Tennessee Walking Horse Museum, in Lynchburg, Tennessee, to find out more about these beautiful horses: www.twhbea.com/twhmuseum.htm

About half a million people visit Virginia every year just to ride or enjoy other horse-related activities. Will you be one of them? Maybe you'll be there in early June, just in time for the Upperville Colt and Horse Show. This show got its start in 1853, which makes it the oldest horse show in the United States. www.upperville.com

Sun, sand, and Chincoteague ponies—what more could a horse-crazy girl want? You'll find them all at Assateague Island National Seashore off Virginia's coast. The ponies roam wild in the woods and on the beach. In midsummer, you can watch the ponies swim across the channel to Chincoteague for Pony Penning Day. There's also a Chincoteague Pony Centre, where you can see ponies up close. www.chincoteague.com/pony/ponies.html

Fans of steeplechasing flock to Middleburg, Virginia, in spring and fall for two big events: The Virginia Gold Cup, a race meet held on the first Saturday in May, and the International Gold Cup, on the third Saturday in October. www.vagoldcup.com

Maryland is also a haven for steeplechasers. One of the biggest races in this state is the four-mile Maryland Hunt Cup, held on the last Saturday in April. www.marylandsteeplechasing.com

Midwestern United States

Head for Mexico—Mexico, Missouri, that is! This town was once known as the "Saddlebred Horse Capital of the World." Today, it's home to the American Saddlebred Horse Museum. www.audrain.org/visitus_saddlebred.html

In St. Louis, Missouri, you can visit Grant's Farm, which breeds horses who may one day be part of a Budweiser Clydesdale hitch. You can even get your photo taken with one of the gentle giants. www.grantsfarm.com/ClydesdaleStables.htm

Horses, horses, and more horses—it must be the Midwest Horse Fair, which takes place in April in Madison, Wisconsin. This fair includes shows, rodeo events, classes on horse topics, and more. www.midwesthorsefair.com

Southwestern United States

You'll find plenty of stables, ranches, rodeos, and horses in the Southwest, where cowpokes still work cattle. You can also spot wild horses there, if you're lucky—especially in Nevada, where half of America's mustangs run free. Find out where by visiting this website first: www.blm.gov/nv/st/en/prog/wh_b.html

Hundreds of horses are on parade every February in Wickenburg, Arizona. They're part of Gold Rush Days, an event that celebrates Arizona's mining history.

You can visit two museums in Texas starring quarter horses. The American Quarter Horse Hall of Fame and Museum is in Amarillo. Its website is www.aqha.com/foundation/museum. The Texas Horse Racing Museum and Hall of Fame in Selma includes other breeds in addition to quarter horses. Visit online at www.txhorseracingmuseumandhalloffame.org

Want to be a cowgirl? Giddy-up to the National Cowgirl Museum and Hall of Fame in Fort Worth, Texas. You can even ride a mechanical bucking bronco while you're there! www.cowgirl.net/default.asp

Western United States

See Seabiscuit's original stall at Santa Anita Park in Arcadia, California, as well as other behind-the-scenes sights, such as the room where silks are kept and the saddling paddock. Just hop aboard the Seabiscuit Tram almost any weekend when racing is underway at the track. You can also visit the track to see morning workouts. Find out more online: www.santaanita.com

Spot Appaloosas at the Appaloosa Museum in Moscow, Idaho. It tells the history of this American breed: www.appaloosamuseum.org

If it's early spring, it's time for the Pendleton Round-Up—a giant rodeo that takes place in Pendleton, Oregon: www.pendletonroundup.com

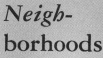

Neighborhoods

Here are some towns in the United States and Canada that have horsey names—though we can't guarantee that they actually have horses!

Bay Horse, MT
Black Horse, PA
Colts Neck, NJ
Deadhorse, AK
Gray Horse, OK
Horse Branch, KY
Horsecamp, ID
Horse Cave, KY
Horse Corner, NH
Horse Creek, WI
Horsefly, B. C.
Horsegall, SC
Horseheads, NY
Horse Heaven, CT
Horse Lake, CA
Horse Landing, MD
Horse Pasture, VA
Hungry Horse, MT
Kicking Horse, MT
New Horse Springs, NM
Old Horse Springs, NM
Spotted Horse, WY
White Horse, NJ
Whitehorse, YT
White Horse Beach, MA
White Horse Farm, DE
Wild Horse, AB
Wild Horse, CO

Oregon also boasts a few herds of wild horses. A corral in Burns, Oregon, is home to mustangs waiting to be adopted, and tours can be arranged if you call ahead of time. Find out more at www.blm.gov/or/districts/burns/wildhorse/corral.php.

Learn about wild horses at the Pryor Mountain Wild Mustang Center in Lovell, Wyoming: www.pryormustangs.org.

The Autry National Center of the American West in Los Angeles, California, includes the Southwest Museum of the American Indian, as well as the Museum of the American West. It's devoted to the history of the western United States and the people who have shaped it. www.autrynationalcenter.org

Everything from alpacas to yaks is on display at the National Western Stock Show in Denver, Colorado, which takes place over the span of several weeks in January. It's one of the world's biggest livestock shows and features classes for horses as well as a rodeo. www.nationalwestern.com/nwss/home/home.php

Canada

The Royal Canadian Mounties are part of Canada's police force. They perform musical rides at fairs and other events in Canada and the United States. You can meet the horses and get a behind-the-scenes tour at the Musical Ride Centre's Rockcliffe Stables in Ottawa, Ontario: www.rcmp-grc.gc.ca/mr-ce/centre-eng.htm#Rockcliffe

The Calgary Stampede is a huge rodeo that rocks Calgary, Alberta, in July: www.calgarystampede.com

You can see beautiful horses compete in show-jumping events nearly year-round at Spruce Meadows, an equine complex in Calgary. Spruce Meadows also hosts other exhibits and events—there's always something going on. Check out their website for more info, as well as an annual Name the Foal Contest! www.sprucemeadows.com

A big horse show is part of the Canadian National Exhibition in late summer, in Toronto. Find out all about "The Ex" at www.theex.com.

The city of Toronto welcomes the countryside every November when the Royal Agricultural Winter Fair arrives, complete with a rodeo and a horse show. www.royalfair.org

Woodbine Racetrack in Toronto, Ontario, boasts the Canadian Horse Racing Hall of Fame. It's devoted to both Thoroughbreds and Standardbreds: www.canadianhorseracinghalloffame.com

Ten Official State Horses

Do you live in one of the ten states that include horses among their state symbols? Check below and see if you do. If not, do a little research on your state and see if you can find a horse breed that's special to it. Is there a breed that played an important role in your state's history? Many state symbols have been chosen thanks to kids who lobbied to make them official. Maybe you can get your class, club, or riding school to mount a horse campaign!

Alabama's state horse is the Racking Horse. This breed is related to the Tennessee Walking Horse. It's known for its natural ability to move smoothly and quickly using a four-beat gait called the "rack." Year selected: 1975.

Idaho's state horse is the Appaloosa. The Nez Perce Indians created this spotted breed more than two hundred years ago. Year selected: 1975.

Kentucky's state horse is the Thoroughbred. This speedball also appears on the Kentucky state quarter. Kentucky is world famous for the Kentucky Derby horse race and Thoroughbred farms. Year selected: 1996.

Maryland's state horse is also the Thoroughbred. This state, like Kentucky, has many Thoroughbred farms as well as an important horse race—the Preakness. Year selected: 2003.

Massachusetts's state horse is the Morgan. All Morgans descend from a little horse called Figure, who was born in Massachusetts in 1789. Year selected: 1970.

Missouri's state horse is the Missouri Fox-trotting Horse. This breed got its start in the state in the 1800s. It "foxtrots" by walking in front and trotting in back. Year selected: 2002.

New Jersey's state animal is simply "the horse"—any breed! The United States Equestrian Team has its headquarters in New Jersey. Year selected: 1970.

North Dakota's state horse is the Nokota Horse. This tough breed descends from horses used by the Sioux Indians. Year selected: 1993.

Tennessee's state horse is the Tennessee Walking Horse. This breed is famous for its smooth strides, which include a gait called the "running walk." Year selected: 2000.

Vermont's state horse is the Morgan. Figure—the horse famous for starting the Morgan breed—lived in Vermont for most of his thirty-two years. Year selected: 1961.

Wah! I Want a Horse!

Okay, so you don't have a horse, and there doesn't seem to be much of a chance of your acquiring one anytime soon. What's a horse-crazy girl to do?

Plenty!

Maybe you've already taken in some of the movies, books, websites, and other horse stuff included in this book. How else can you get even more horsepower into your life?

Horse Courses

The best "horse course," of course, is a horse camp or a series of riding lessons. You've probably already discussed these dreams with your parents. Perhaps you're even saving up babysitting money or allowance so that you can go to a camp or take lessons.

But you can also find horse activities tucked into other programs that aren't dedicated solely to horses. Take 4-H, for example. That community got its start in rural areas and focused on agriculture; today, even kids in cities can join 4-H.

Have a look at a 4-H show by visiting a site called "4-H Horse Farm": ext.vt.edu/resources/4h/virtualfarm/equine/equine.html. Look for the link called "horse show," and you can watch movies of 4-H riders in action.

Other organizations for kids also have horse programs. Many Girl Scout and Camp Fire councils, for example, offer horse programs—either at their own campgrounds or local stables.

Pony Club, of course, is devoted to horses. (You can join a Pony Club even if you don't have a horse, but you do need to be able to borrow one to use on occasion.) Find out more about Pony Club at www.ponyclub.org (if you live in the U.S.A.) or www.canadianponyclub.org (if you live in Canada).

Another organization, the National FFA, is devoted to agricultural science education and offers programs to help young people who want to pursue careers with horses. One program, Horse Evaluation, not only acquaints students with horses and horse careers but also gives them the opportunity to compete in teams at Career Development Events. Teams are tested on their knowledge of horses using both written and oral exams. Students also judge real horses and explain their decision making. Find out more about the National FFA Organization at www.ffa.org.

Volunteering

You've probably read horse stories in which girls show up at stables and convince the owners to let them hang around and help out in exchange for riding their horses. This is an adventure you're most likely to encounter only in stories.

Why? Because in real life, in modern times, stable owners could get into a heap of costly trouble if they let people near their horses and those people get hurt. (That's why you have to sign a form before going on a trail ride or taking lessons. The form says that you know horseback riding can be risky, and you won't blame the stable if you get hurt.)

But if a stable actually has a volunteer program in place, then you really can make this storybook plot come true. Some riding stables, for example, train their students to become volunteer stable helpers. These kids can swap stable chores for extra riding time. If you get a chance to take riding lessons and are interested in doing work like this, ask about it before you decide on a stable. Be sure to ask what age you need to be to start volunteering.

Here's another idea: Is there a zoo or farm-related park in your area that has pony rides for kids? You may be too old to ride the little ponies, but you may be just the right age to help lead ponies, clean tack, and muck out stalls! Some

HELP A HORSE

Did you know that you can "sponsor" a horse at a horse-rescue sanctuary? A sponsor sends money to help pay for the care and feeding of a particular horse. Sometimes girls use their allowances and babysitting money to sponsor a horse. A Girl Scout troop, 4-H club, or other organized group might team up to support a horse, too.

Horses end up at sanctuaries for many reasons. Sometimes horses are surrendered to a sanctuary by people who can no longer care for them, just as dogs and cats are brought to animal shelters. Sometimes horses are rescued from situations in which they are being neglected or abused. And sometimes sanctuaries include retired animals, such as ex-racehorses. Some unwanted horses have even been rescued after they have been sold for slaughter.

You can find a horse-rescue organization in your area using an online horse dictionary such as "O Horse," which can be found at this site: **www.ohorse.com/organizations/horse-rescue.** You can also search online using "horse rescue" and the name of your state or province as the search terms.

pony-ride sites also have links to local organizations, such as 4-H, to draw in kids who can help with chores in exchange for learning how to care for and handle horses.

A horse-rescue group might also be eager to have young helpers around the barn. You can find out about horse-rescue groups in your area by doing a search for "horse rescue," "horse retirement," or "horse sanctuary" along with the name of your state or province. You can also contact The American Horse Council for information (**www.horsecouncil.org**). The Unwanted Horse Coalition (**www.unwantedhorsecoalition.org**) also has good advice about scoping out such horse facilities to make sure they take good care of the animals.

Therapeutic riding stables, which enable people with physical and mental disabilities to ride, also use helpers. If you'd like to volunteer at a therapeutic riding center, visit the website of the North American Riding for the Handicapped Association at **www.narha.org**. Click on the "Find a Center" button, and use the interactive form to find centers in your state or province. Then visit the website of a center to find out about its volunteer program.

Sophie Says: I take riding lessons at a stable. I've also become a volunteer at the stable. I help tack up horses, groom them, feed them, muck paddocks, and help with lessons and camps. I get rewarded by a free hour and 45 minutes of riding! In my riding lessons, I have learned so much. You tack up your own horse, groom it, and take it to the arena. You are in charge of your own horse. My teacher is the greatest! She helps everyone so much, and is really patient. She is one of my favorite people on earth! Riding lessons are a really fun way to spend time with horses and learn to ride, even if you don't have a horse of your own.

HEY!

Don't forget to check with your parents once you've got the info you need to track down volunteer opportunities.

When I Grow Up, I Want to Be . . .

How do YOU finish that sentence?

If you're like a lot of horse girls, you may fill in the blank with a job that relates to horses. Maybe you want to ride show jumpers. Or be a jockey. Perhaps you want to be a trainer, a groom, or a horse doctor. Maybe you want to have a job that's got nothing to do with horses, but one that definitely leaves you with enough time and money to have a horse.

It's fun to ponder what you might be when you grow up—and how to work horses into the mix. Here are some of the many horse careers you can pursue to inspire your daydreaming.

If you like caring for horses, you could be—

◆ A groom at a racing stable, breeding farm, or other horse business
◆ A hot walker, who leads horses around to cool them off after a race or other event
◆ A farrier, who shoes horses and helps fix their foot and leg problems

If you love to ride, you could be—

◆ A professional rider who rides other people's horses (there are plenty of horse lovers who own jumpers, hunters, dressage, and other horses that they either can't ride or don't want to ride, but are eager to show)
◆ An exercise rider who exercises horses for a stable or at a racetrack
◆ A guide for a trail-riding outfit or a dude ranch
◆ A "pony rider"—the person who rides a "pony" (non-racehorse) while leading a racehorse to the starting gate
◆ An "outrider"—the person on horseback at a racetrack who leads all the racehorses and their "ponies" to the starting gate and also catches any horses that run away

If you like to teach, you could be—

♦A horse trainer who teaches young horses their manners and some basic rules

♦A horse trainer who teaches horses in certain disciplines, such as dressage or for performing in movies

♦A "horse whisperer"—a trainer whose specialty is reading a horse's body language and communicating with it; often such a trainer works with young, untrained horses or horses who have been abused

♦A riding instructor who teaches kids to ride

If you like science a lot, you could be—

♦A veterinarian who specializes in treating horses (becoming a vet includes four years of college and four years of veterinary school)

♦A veterinary assistant or technician, who works with an equine veterinarian

♦A horse dentist

♦A scientist who researches horse diseases, horse behavior, how horses have changed over time, how wild horses affect the land they live on . . . you name it!

♦A breeder who figures out which horses to match up to produce foals who'll be the best runners, or jumpers, or barrel racers . . .

Find Out More

Get the scoop on horse careers by trotting online to this American Youth Horse Council Web page: **ayhc.com/resources.htm**. Then scroll down to the link called "Horse Career Possibilities" and click on it. It'll take you to a brochure that lists many jobs related to horses and how to find them.

You can also learn more about horse careers at your library. You can search the catalog for books or ask a librarian to help. Doing this will turn up books such as *50 Careers with Horses! From Accountant to Wrangler* by Bonnie Kreitler.

If you like math a lot, you could be—

♦An accountant who keeps track of expenses for a trainer, a breeder, or other horse person

♦A builder or architect who specializes in planning and building stables and other structures for horses

♦A "clocker"—the person who keeps track of how far and how fast horses run as they work out on a racetrack in the morning, then reports this information to officials at the track

♦The manager or owner of a tack shop

If you're really organized, with great attention to detail, and good at keeping others organized, you could be—

◆A judge at a horse show or rodeo

◆An assistant for a professional in the horse world—for example, a jockey's agent (the person who lines up rides for the jockey)

◆A racetrack steward, who watches races and makes sure that all rules are followed

◆A "horse identifier"—the person who checks a racehorse's lip tattoo, colors, markings, and the like to make sure it matches up with the horse's papers, so that the right horse is heading for the starting gate

If you like to write, draw, or do other creative or crafty kinds of work, you could be—

◆A saddler, who designs and makes tack for horses

◆A clothes designer who comes up with stunning show outfits

◆A writer who works for newspapers and magazines about horses or who writes books about them

◆An artist who paints portraits of horses for their owners or makes sculptures of horses

◆A designer who thinks up designs for stuffed or plastic toy horses

◆A game designer who thinks up great horse games for girls to play on computers

◆An illustrator who makes posters, cards, or other images of horses for horse-crazy girls to collect, or who illustrates books about horses (like this one)

HORSE COLLEGE

Jockey Chris McCarron got his start as a "hot walker" in 1971. His first mount in a race, in 1974, finished last. He went on to become a leading jockey, with victories in big races such as the Kentucky Derby. His career inspired him to start the North American Racing Academy (NARA) in Lexington, Kentucky. Students at NARA learn how to be race riders and also how to care for and train racehorses. You can find out more online at **http://nara.kctcs.edu.**

Horse Girls with Heart

Every horse girl has a dream. Her dream may be to own a horse, or just to learn to ride one. She may dream of helping horses by being a vet or running a sanctuary. She may dream of passing on her own love of horses by teaching kids to work with horses. Just like horses themselves, dreams come in many shapes and sizes.

As you get older, your dreams will grow and change, too. You'll shape them as you discover new ideas, learn new facts, and toss out old notions. You'll mix them up with new interests and ambitions.

As you follow your dream, you might meet a few people who'll try to tell you your dream is impossible, or that you're "limiting" yourself by sticking to horses. They'll tell you not to read so many horse books, or that "there's more to life than horses."

But as you know from reading this book—and other horse books—humans and horses share a long history. Horses are linked to many of the subjects you learn about in school and that you'll keep learning about throughout your life: history, literature, technology, science, art.

They can also take you places you might never have explored otherwise. So hang in there. Who knows what trails your horse dreams will follow!

Horse Girls Rock!

Every horse girl has a story—and here are a few we think you'll find inspiring. These girls have fun with horses, but they also know it takes hard work, dedication, perseverance, and guts to become a horsewoman.

It's Good for a Girl, Too!

Winston Churchill was the prime minister of Great Britain during the 1940s and 1950s. One of his famous sayings is, "There's something about the outside of a horse that is good for the inside of a man."

Sara Wiebke

Sara Wiebke fell in love with horses when she was six. That's when she met the gentle horses who lived next door to her aunt in Georgia. She learned to ride, then started showing. But by the time she was twelve, Sara had a new venture: working at a horse rescue.

Like all horse rescues, Pure Thoughts Horse and Foal Rescue in Loxahatchee, Florida, depends on volunteers to help care for and train their horses. Some of the horses are scared, sad horses who've been abused and need to learn to trust people again. Others are horses retired from racing. There are even "babies"—unwanted foals rescued from breeding operations.

One of Sara's first "students" was a young pinto pony named Yahzi. The two have appeared in magazines such as *Young Rider* and *American Girl* to champion rescue horses. Sara has also gotten friends involved. www.purethoughtshorserescue.com

Brittany Rostron

Brittany Rostron was only sixteen when she started rescuing horses that were going to be shipped off to slaughterhouses. She called her program Project SAGE Horse Rescue, after her own well-loved rescued horse, Sage.

Since Brittany founded SAGE in 2007, she's rescued more than thirty horses. The horses are cared for, or "fostered," by volunteers at different farms on Long Island in New York, where SAGE is based.

Brittany began riding when she was about five years old. She's now hard at work seven days a week helping to care for and train her rescue horses to get them ready for adoption into "forever homes." Brittany also holds fundraisers to raise money for the horses' upkeep. You can find out more about SAFE on Brittany's website at http://projectsagehorserescue.org.

Hannah Tarwater

Mucking stalls. Brushing horses. Seeing miracles daily. It was all in a day's work for twelve-year-old Hannah Tarwater, who volunteered at Helping Hands Therapeutic Riding Center in Kansas City, Missouri.

Therapeutic riding uses horsepower to help people with disabilities. Riding a horse can help a person with muscle weakness, for example, build up strength that can help them sit up or even walk on their own.

Hannah helped out with barn chores, such as mucking stalls and grooming. She also led mounted horses and worked as a "sidewalker," helping to support the rider. The effect that riding has on the students amazed Hannah every week.

If you'd like to volunteer at a therapeutic riding center, visit the website of the North American Riding for the Handicapped Association at www.narha.org. Click on the "Find a Center" button and use the interactive form to find centers in your state or province. Then visit the website of a center to find out about its volunteer program.

Bibliography

I used many sources to research info about horses for this book: websites, magazines, newspaper articles old and new, and, of course, other books. Some of these sources are mentioned in *For Horse-Crazy Girls Only*. Websites, for example, are noted in many parts of this book. So are some of the books. Here, you'll find more info about those books, namely who published them and when. This info is useful because you might need it, say, if a book is old and you want your local library to try to find it from another library for you. I've also tossed in some other books that I found really useful and interesting but aren't mentioned elsewhere in *Horse-Crazy*.

FICTION

Aldridge, James. *A Sporting Proposition*. Boston: Little, Brown & Co., 1973.

Amateau, Gigi. *Chancey of the Maury River*. Cambridge, MA: Candlewick Press, 2008.

Bagnold, Enid. *National Velvet*. New York: HarperCollins, 2002.

Brown, Frieda Kenyon. *Last Hurdle*. North Haven, CT: Linnet Books, 1998.

Doty, Jean Slaughter. *If Wishes Were Horses*. New York: Atheneum, 1984.

—. *Summer Pony*. New York: Collier Books, 1973.

—. *Winter Pony*. New York: Macmillan, 1975.

Farley, Walter. *The Black Stallion*. New York: Random House, 1991.

Ferguson, Ruby. *Jill's Gymkhana*. Edinburgh: Fidra Books, 2009.

Grew, David. *Beyond Rope and Fence*. New York: Boni & Liveright, 1922.

Haas, Jessie. *Birthday Pony*. New York: HarperCollins, 2004.

—. *Runaway Radish*. New York: Greenwillow Books, 2001.

Harlow, Joan Hiatt. *Midnight Rider*. New York: Aladdin, 2006.

Hart, Alison. *Gabriel's Horses*. Atlanta: Peachtree Publishers, 2008.

Henry, Marguerite. *King of the Wind*. Chicago: Rand McNally & Co., 1948.

—. *Misty of Chincoteague*. Chicago: Rand McNally & Co., 1947.

—. *Mustang: Wild Spirit of the West*. Chicago: Rand McNally & Co., 1966.

—. *Sea Star, Orphan of Chincoteague*. Chicago: Rand McNally & Co., 1949.

—. *Stormy, Misty's Foal*. Chicago: Rand McNally & Co., 1963.

—. *White Stallions of Lipizza*. Chicago: Rand McNally & Co., 1964.

James, Will. *Smoky the Cowhorse*. New York: Aladdin, 2008.

Lee, Jared. *I'm at the End of My Rope and You're Tugging on It*. Lebanon, OH: Red Pony Press, 2004.

—. *Talk to the Hoof*. Lebanon, OH: Red Pony Press, 2000.

Morpurgo, Michael. *War Horse*. New York: Scholastic, 2006.

O'Hara, Maureen. *Green Grass of Wyoming*. New York: Lippincott, 1946.

—. *My Friend Flicka*. New York: Lippincott, 1941.

—. *Thunderhead*. New York: Lippincott, 1943.

Pullein-Thompson, Christine. *It Began with Picotee*. London: A & C Black, 1946.

Ryan, Pam Muñoz. *Paint the Wind*. New York: Scholastic, 2007.

Sewell, Anna. *Black Beauty*. New York: Sterling Publishing Co., 2004.

Wedekind, Annie. *A Horse of Her Own*. New York: Macmillan, 2009.

—. *Little Prince: The Story of a Shetland Pony*. New York: Macmillan, 2009.

—. *Wild Blue: The Story of a Mustang Appaloosa*. New York: Macmillan, 2009.

NONFICTION

Encyclopedias, Dictionaries, and Other All-about-Horses Books

Broom, David. *Encyclopedia of the Horse*. San Diego: Thunder Bay Press, 1998.

Burns, Deborah, ed. *Storey's Horse-Lover's Encyclopedia*. North Adams, MA: Storey Publishing, LLC., 2001.

Clutton-Brock, Juliet. *Horse*. New York: Alfred A. Knopf, 1992.

Curry, Marion. *1,000 Facts on Horses*. New York: Barnes & Noble Books, 2004.

Dossenbach, Monique and Hans D. *The Noble Horse*. New York: Portland House, 1987.

Draper, Judith, Debby Sly, and Sarah Muir. *Complete Book of Horses and Riding*. New York: Barnes & Noble Books, 2003.

Dutson, Judith. *Storey's Illustrated Guide to 96 Horse Breeds of North America*. North Adams, MA: Storey Publishing LLC., 2005.

Eby, Vivienne M. *The Horse Dictionary*. Jefferson, NC: McFarland & Co., 1995.

Edwards, Elwyn Hartley. *The New Encyclopedia of the Horse*. New York: Dorling Kindersley, 2001.
—. *The Ultimate Horse Book*. New York: Dorling Kindersley, 1991.
Harris, Moira C. *America's Horses*. Guilford, CT: The Lyons Press, 2003.
Henry, Marguerite. *Album of Horses*. Chicago: Rand McNally, 1951.
Kimball, Cheryl. *The Complete Horse*. St. Paul, MN: Voyageur Press, 2006.
Mitchum, Petrine Day, and Audrey Pavia. *Hollywood Hoofbeats*. Irvine, CA: Bowtie Press, 2005.
Pickeral, Tamsin. *The Encyclopedia of Horses and Ponies*. Bath: Parragon Publishing, 2004.
Ransford, Sandy. *Horse and Pony Breeds*. Boston: Kingfisher Books Ltd., 2003.
Seggerman, Sheri, and Mary Tiegreen. *1,001 Reasons to Love Horses*. New York: Stewart, Tabori & Chang, 2005.
Whitaker, Julie. *The Horse: A Miscellany of Equine Knowledge*. New York: St. Martin's Press, 2007.
The Visual Dictionary of the Horse. New York: Dorling Kindersley Limited, 1994.

Books about Horse Behavior
Budiansky, Stephen. *The Nature of Horses*. New York: Simon & Schuster Inc., 1997.
Crisp, Marty. *Everything Horse*. Minnetonka, MN: NorthWord, 2005.
Dines, Lisa. *Why Horses Do That*. Minocqua, WI: Willow Creek Press, 2003.
Hill, Cherry. *How to Think Like a Horse*. North Adams, MA: Storey Publishing, 2006.
McBane, Susan. *How Your Horse Works*. Devon, UK: David & Charles, 1999.

Books about Riding and Horse Care
Bird, Jo. *Keeping a Horse the Natural Way*. Hauppauge, NY: Barrons's Education Series, Inc., 2002.
Davis, Caroline. *The Young Equestrian*. Buffalo, NY: Firefly Books Inc., 2000.
Decaire, Camela, and Michelle Watkins, eds. *Girls and Their Horses*. Middleton, WI: American Girl Publishing Inc., 2006.
Dickins, Rosie, and Gill Harvey. *Usborne Little Book of Riding & Pony Care*. London: Usborne Publishing Ltd., 2003.
Draper, Judith. *My First Horse and Pony Book*. Boston: Kingfisher, 2005.
Henderson, Carolyn. *A Young Rider's Guide: Learn to Ride*. New York: Dorling Kindersley, 2005.
Kidd, Jane, ed. *Learning to Ride*. New York: Macmillan, 1992.
Lewis, Charni. *Braiding Manes and Tails*. North Adams, MA: Storey Publishing, 2008.
Pinch, Dorothy Henderson. *Happy Horsemanship*. New York: Fireside, 1998.
Ransford, Sandy. *First Riding Lessons*. Boston: Kingfisher Books Ltd., 2004.
—. *Horse and Pony Care*. Boston: Kingfisher Books Ltd., 2004.
Vogel, Colin. *Complete Horse Care Manual*. New York: Dorling Kindersley, 2003.

Books about Wild Horses
Dines, Lisa. *The American Mustang Guidebook*. Minocqua, WI: Willow Creek Press, 2001.
Edwards, Elwyn Hartley. *Wild Horses: The World's Last Surviving Herds*. Irvington, NY: Hylas Publishing, 2003.
Halls, Kelly Milner. *Wild Horses: Galloping Through Time*. Plain City, OH: Darby Creek Publishing, 2008.
Hyde, Dayton O. *All the Wild Horses*. St. Paul, MN: Voyageur Press, 2006.
Kirkpatrick, Jay F. *Into the Wind: Wild Horses of North America*. Minocqua, WI: Northword Press, Inc., 1994.
Pomeranz, Lynne. *Among Wild Horses*. North Adams, MA: Storey Publishing, 2006.
Pomerantz, Rich. *Wild Horses of the Dunes*. Philadelphia: Running Press, 2004.
Ryden, Hope. *Wild Horses I Have Known*. New York: Clarion Books, 1999.
Scott, Traer. *Wild Horses: Endangered Beauty*. London: Merrell Publishers Ltd., 2008.

Books about Collecting, Drawing, and Working with Horses
Baskett, John. *The Horse in Art*. New Haven: Yale University Press, 2006.
Browell, Felicia. *Breyer Animal Collector's Guide*. Paducah, KY: Collector Books, 2007.
Evers, June. *Anyone Can Draw Horses!* Goshen, NY: Horse Hollow Press, 2003.
Kreitler, Bonnie. *50 Careers with Horses! From Accountant to Wrangler*. Emmaus, PA: Breakthrough Publications, 2006.
Pickeral, Tamsin. *The Horse: 30,000 Years of the Horse in Art*. London: Merrell Publishers, 2009.
Savitt, Sam. *Draw Horses with Sam Savitt*. Boonsboro, MD: Half Halt Press, 1991.
Young, Nancy Atkinson. *Breyer Molds & Models*. Atglen, PA: Schiffer Publishing, 1998.

Index